Volume 6, Number 4, 2019

Southern Europe in the Mediterranean Context

Special Issue edited by **Teresa de Noronha** and **Eric Vaz**

Table of Contents

This special issue on "Southern Europe in the Mediterranean Context" is edited by Teresa de Noronha (University of Algarve, Faro, Portugal) and Eric Vaz (Ryerson University, Toronto, Canada). With the exception of the editorial, all contributions to this special issue have already been published in earlier issues of REGION, for the sake of immediate exposure of the content.

- *Integrated local development in Mediterranean marginal territories: The case study of Casentino (Italy), Algarve (Portugal) and Corse (France)* by Andrea Ricci, Mario Biggeri and Andrea Ferrannini was originally published in vol. 6, no. 1, 1–16.

- *Rehabilitation and Renewal of Mediterranean Structures. The Utopic Landscape of Algarve* by Carlos Bragança dos Santos was originally published in vol. 5, no. 1, 113–135.

- *The role of the European Union on immigration. An anthropological approach to the treaties that have been carried out in Europe in order to manage diversity* by Carmen Clara Bravo Torres was originally published in vol. 6, no. 1, 45–53.

- *The Mediterranean Variety of Capitalism, Flexibility of Work Schedules, and Labour Productivity in Southern Europe* by Alberto Vallejo-Peña and Sandro Giachi was originally published in vol. 5, no. 3, 21–38.

- *Similitudes and singularities of higher education systems in the Mediterranean countries: Historical construction, policy and evolution of key indicators* by Cláudia Urbano was originally published in vol. 6, no. 1, 25–44.

- *The Mediterranean Diet and the Increasing Demand of the Olive Oil Sector: Shifts and Environmental Consequences* by Bruno Neves and Iva Miranda Pires was originally published in vol. 5, no. 1, 101–112.

REGION, The journal of ERSA / Powered by WU
ISSN: 2409-5370, ISBN: 978-3-9504846-4-9

ERSA: http://www.ersa.org
WU: http://www.wu.ac.at

Editorials

REGION

The Journal of ERSA
Powered by WU

Volume 6, Number 4, 2019, E1–E5
DOI: 10.18335/region.v6i4.280

journal homepage: region.ersa.org

Why a multidisciplinary agenda for Southern Europe?

Teresa de Noronha[1]**, Eric Vaz**[2]

[1] University of Algarve, Faro, Portugal
[2] Ryerson University, Toronto, Canada

Received: 18 September 2019/Accepted: 18 September 2019

Since the process of Southern Europe's integration in the European Union, the Mediterranean region has seen a more considerable gap between central and northern European countries and its Southern European counterpart. Thus, in a European context of social cohesion, it becomes necessary to better understand Southern Europe, without escaping to the common perception of the complexity of Mediterranean culture. As a significant player throughout history, Southern Europe consistently established a platform of diversity and freedom, bringing peace between different historic-cultural traditions. Moreover, the southern frontier of Europe to Africa and Asia has become a crucial determinant in the current times of change. Where ruptures in the political systems are also defining new patterns of regional migration. Meanwhile, the integration of Italy, Portugal, Spain, and Greece into the European Union reinforced an essential search for stability, altering to some extent the political and economic predispositions of these countries. This has been followed by somewhat rigid institutions, that remain, to a certain extent, an obstacle to sustainable development, and justify a broader assessment of the potential of policy and governance intervention. In the Mediterranean region stagnation, or increasing poverty, and migration is leading the most impoverished areas to a deleterious deprivation of human resources and capital. Southern European countries may represent a bridging alternative and an exemplar representation of democracy. A positive Mediterranean agenda is necessary, where migration patterns become a substantial factor in the future of all the frontier countries: Italy and Greece, Spain, and Portugal. This special issue collects recent insights in socio-economic developments in Mediterranean countries in order to further a future agenda for Southern Europe.

The future agenda for Southern Europe is multidimensional and requires a multidisciplary approach. Three main dimensions need to be covered by such an agenda: (i) Migrations patterns, whereby sociological and economic aspects take into account the diverse territorial areas and individual regions; (ii) Sustainable economic transitions that cater to better and more integrative business structures; (iii) Entrepreneurship and creativity, where management of scarce natural and financial resources is pursued to suitably create new productive and networking systems, which actively absorb diversified populations in a multicultural and pluralist Europe.

The proposals of the Action Plan on the integration of third-country nationals (European Commission 2016) reinforces the existing "evolutional process". This includes the need for integration policies directed towards local characteristics that promote access to services, education, and jobs. Southern Europe, in the Mediterranean context, is part of an extended effort to discuss, for the first time, this pluralistic agenda. It outlines the complex aspects of southern Europe, which require a significant reflection about the Mediterranean region and the European countries within it. Notably, the region's cultural and populational background. In a forthcoming monograph titled *Southern*

Europe – Major Trends and New Prospects (Vaz, de Noronha 2020), the authors Eric Vaz and Teresa de Noronha unravel the complexity of southern Europe's integration from a regional science perspective and discuss these issues from a geographical and economic viewpoint.

Driven by the interest triggered through this contribution, the authors organized a major international conference, entitled "Mediterranean Cultures and Societies" in 2017, at the Research Centre of Spatial and Organizational Dynamics, University of the Algarve, Portugal, in partnership with the ICSR Mediterranean Knowledge, Italy. The high quality of presented papers became a cradle for a broader spectrum of different scholarly contributions within the socio-economic problems of Southern Europe. These contributions have led to the following publication outputs:

1. *Historical Contexts and Identities of the Mediterranean Countries*, published in the Journal of Spatial and Organizational Dynamics (de Noronha, Mangone 2018), is a collection of eight papers discussing, from a geographical and sociological perspective, case studies related to Mediterranean identities in Southern Europe.

2. *The Mediterranean and Migrations*, in the Journal of Mediterranean Knowledge (de Noronha 2018), advances some historical and sociological theoretical considerations of what remains one of the greatest challenges of the 21st century for Mediterranean and Europe –migration.

3. Finally, this publication, *Southern Europe in the Mediterranean Context* in REGION, calls for multidisciplinary aspects suggesting that regional advances in development and sustainability of the region can only occur if a multidisciplinary approach is used.

One of the primary goals of this recently developed research is to call awareness to the need for increasing proximity between the Mediterranean countries and the rest of Europe. The distance grew through the modernization process of the 1950s and the post-colonial policies of the last century. This process was, at least partially, responsible for the communities integrating external forms of modernity without adding new developments in the process of growth and economic valorisation.

Meanwhile, over the last three decades, the European Union had a significant role in shaping the decision-making processes on economic growth and development across all its member states. However, a growing gap between Northern and Southern Europe has been recognized. Not only did the last international economic recession have negative impacts on Southern European countries but also some profound structural adjustments within Southern European countries occured.

The significant impact of the last economic recession (2008) on sustainable development was felt strongly at a geographical level. While infrastructures built during the nineties still exist in many places, their upkeep and maintenance have become condemned for future generations. Meanwhile, the available policy support and investment in research and development became restricted. This led to some apathy by decision-makers who lacked financial possibilities to invest and maintain the status quo of regions. For example, monitoring initiatives by the European Environmental Agency have shown a paramount increase in urban sprawl in southern Europe, leading to a direct depletion of resources resulting from ineffective planning in the last decades. This takes its toll directly on land use and infrastructure, leaving decision-makers incapacitated to cope with the current crisis.

Surprisingly, and out of a context of adversity, in Portugal and Spain conditions for economic growth and remarkably creative solutions for sustainability are emerging . This shows Southern Europe's resilience, the capacity of innovation, and its historical driving force to face challenges and find new paths to growth and prosperity. From its struggle, many socio-economic examples may be observed, and its heritage and challenges should motivate scholars to further regional research on its challenges.

The objective of this publication is to emphasize a continuous stream of research topics related to the complexity of Southern Europe's economic structures, urban and climate change impacts, urban sprawl and natural heritage across Portugal, Spain, Italy, and

Greece. We are optimistic that it is through regional science and location-based research that a unique laboratory is formed that may offer innovative solutions to address complex change in national governance post-crises. We are delighted to bring this paradigm to Southern Europe. Many examples of resilience of territories could be added, and remarkable findings on the history of adaptation and economic growth.

This editorial justifies the need to tackle the current situation in Southern Europe from a multidisciplinary perspective. The ubiquitous nature of regional and urban planning has led to the development of a series of instruments and frameworks, embodied in the local policy agendas of Southern European countries. The tools available and digital instruments such as land use and land cover assessments have become crucial instruments to monitor the inevitable change of the rapidly transitioning environments. It is in the reinvention of public space and landscape that the articulation of urban fabric must take place to offer an integrative vision of future sustainability. Such integrative visions call for multidisciplinary actions to understand the context of regions and policy, as well as multi-tiered scales and methods to foster sustainable development of Southern Europe. It is evident that there is still a debate on what is the best approach to improve development in Southern Europe. However, it is through the incorporation of geographical analysis that one can better frame the multidisciplinary actions towards resilience of landscape. Further contributions to an interdisciplinary agenda in Southern Europe enable the efficient detection of the sustainability of urban regions in the South. Thus, leading to proactive action taking advantage of spatial analysis, GIS, and regional science.

The first article in this special issue *"Integrated local development in Mediterranean marginal territories: The case study of Casentino (Italy), Algarve (Portugal) and Corse (France)"* by Andrea Ricci, Mario Biggeri and Andrea Ferrannini present three case studies across Italy, Portugal, and France to propose lessons learned from a long-term development process at the local level. Today, marginalized Mediterranean territories are facing tremendous challenges but at the same time they have relevant endogenous resources, which are often underutilized and unexploited. In the last decades, they have been characterized by a progressive abandonment in favour of urban areas, with consequent high social costs such as the hydrogeological instability, land degradation, and soil erosion. The paper aims to verify the idea that Mediterranean peripheries, , could take part in the formation of their own development trajectories. Additionally, that these territories can actively contribute to the harmonious development of Europe, creating new jobs opportunities and stable development patterns. The structure of this paper starts with general theoretical arguments and a short description of European policies for development. Then, it follows with a diagnostic analysis of three local territorial contexts – i.e. Casentino (Italy), Algarve (Portugal) and Corse (France). Finally, it returns to the general European issues and proposes implications as well as lessons learnt in the analysis of the development processes at the local level.

The second contribution, *"Rehabilitation and Renewal of Mediterranean Structures. The Utopic Landscape of Algarve"* by Carlos Bragança dos Santos, explores features of Mediterranean landscapes and their relationship to identity in a context of coastal zones with intense human impact. The author interrelates ecological, aesthetic, symbolic, socio-economic, and political aspects that influence the spatial distribution of structures. Additionally, the author considers/analyzes the image of the terraces as a typical geographic feature of southern European regions. One of the remarkable features of Mediterranean landscapes is the terraced landscape, usually supported by dry stone walling. The terraces, property division walls, pathways, and traditional paths create network compartmentalization that define landscape identity. The informational content, aesthetic quality, ecological, and cultural values allowed by this articulated construction are particularly important in coastal zones with intense human impact. On the Algarve, the hills displayed by such structures are the background to an urban-touristic system. The values that local people may assign to their landscapes will determine the acknowledgment of the structural elements under analysis, but the role of tourists must also be seriously considered. Beyond nostalgic solutions, one must prospect the future of the dry-stone walling structure into the diversity of possible solutions for a sustainable landscape development, which enhances the living part of an inseparable unit that includes the densest urbanized areas with less ecological functions.

The third article, *"The role of the European Union on immigration. An anthropological approach to the treaties that have been carried out in Europe in order to manage diversity"* by Carmen Clara Bravo Torres, brings us to one of the greatest sociological concerns facing Southern Europe recently – migrations. Specifically, this is achieved through an analysis of how EU agreements are not adapted to the emerging migration settings. Migrations are a global phenomenon that has prevailed throughout history. In the last decades, there is a need to control every person who enters and leaves the borders of a country. This fact can be observed in the European Union where, at least, during the last decade, the migratory phenomenon is considered a problem. The EUcarries out different measures to manage this diversity within its borders. However, these measurements are not adapted to the different contexts and are not carried out by all the countries within the EU. Despite all this, the discourse used by the European Comission promotes European identity ahead of the rest, differentiating those who are considered others. These themes are studied in this paper, which will allow readers to understand what treaties have been established in the European Union regarding migration and how national diversity is managed through them.

"The Mediterranean Variety of Capitalism, Flexibility of Work Schedules, and Labour Productivity in Southern Europe" is the fourth article in this special issue. Alberto Vallejo Peña and Sandro Giachi highlight the existence of diverse institutional models of work organization between geographical areas of Europe and compare the situation of four representative countries of southern Europe with that of the rest of Europe. Their conclusions may surprise. Sociology has long been used to highlight the existence of diverse institutional models of work organization between geographical areas of Europe. Based on this, to compare the situation of four representative countries of southern Europe (Spain, Italy, Greece and Portugal) with that of the rest of Europe is proposed. Specifically, through addressing the number of hours worked and the flexibility of working hours as key elements of their institutional model of work organisation, as well as their impact on levels of labour productivity. Taking the model of the varieties of capitalism as a reference, this study compares the behaviour of the Mediterranean (Southern European) countries with other European regions. Indicators have been obtained from the year 2010 and 2015 datasets of the European Work Conditions Survey (EWCS). Including the number of hours worked, the flexibility in the hours of entry and exit, and the tendency to work the same number of hours per day. After comparing averages in both sets and applying linear regressions, the following conclusions have been reached: (1) Productivity in Southern countries is on a par with the European average but far from the more corporatist and liberal (Northern European) areas; (2) the South maintains a high average of hours worked (above the European average) to compensate for the poor productivity of its hours; and (3) the incorporation of flexible schedules is associated with elevated levels of productivity.

In *"Similitudes and singularities of higher education systems in the Mediterranean countries: Historical construction, policy and evolution of key indicators"*, Cláudia Urbano finds that Southern Europe has been presenting many differences with the rest of the continent to ensure comparability of the standards and quality of higher education qualifications. Additionally, Urbano confirms that education in such countries needs strengthening by introducing sustainable development, through a holistic approach, into educational curricula, from primary school to higher education. Knowledge management issues are a high priority topic for growth enhancement in Southern Europe. Thus, we are witnessing a need for a quick and intelligent reaction from organizations to expedite change. Higher education is one of the most important values for changes in societies and exchanges among different societies. Analysing higher education systems in Europe, Southern Europe has been deviating from the rest of the continent, despite the effort of the Bologna Process to ensure comparability in the standards and quality of higher education qualifications. Considering four Southern Europe countries – Portugal, Spain, Italy and Greece – and their link to a certain Mediterranean culture, our proposal is to analyse these countries' higher education systems and their economic state. This can be achieved using indicators on educational stock, economic growth, income distribution, supply and demand of higher education and economic indicators relating training and the economy such as graduated employment rates. Also, education public policies will be considered in the analysis as they shape higher education systems' trajectories. Comparing them, we can identify similitudes and singularities in these education systems, leading us to conclude about the existence of a Southern European approach to making higher education a specific value in Mediterranean culture. This topic is even more important as it may be related to the recent focus of EU activities in the Southern Mediterranean region. The Mediterranean Strategy for Sustainable Development (MSSD) recognises that education in the Mediterranean needs strengthening by introducing sustainable development, through a holistic approach, into educational curricula, from primary school to higher education.

Finally, the sixth contribution, *"The Mediterranean Diet and the Increasing Demand of the Olive Oil Sector: Shifts and Environmental Consequences"*, by Bruno Neves and Iva Miranda Pires, tackles one of the most interesting topics of the region's traditions and contributions for social wellbeing, diet. Mediterranean countries play a crucial role as olive oil producers and consumers compared to other world regions. This work focuses on the development of world production, trade and consumption in olive oil. The Mediterranean region stands out from both the rest of the world and the Northern European countries with respect to olive oil production and consumption. Aspects such as communicating the the benefits of a Mediterranean diet, the Slow Food Movement, the International Olive Council campaigns, and the successive Common Agricultural Policies are discussed. Such increases and stimuli brought, and is still bringing, changes to the olive oil sector. Notably, a shifting tendency in production modes as well as modernization of the sector in response to the increasing demand. Such changes are altering landscapes and are considered environmentally harmful to the ecosystems because the production process is shifting to more intensive methods and monoculture plantations.

Much remains to be explored in our research agenda that has not yet been assessed. Our efforts were supported by the interest in this fascinating region, its history, its identities, its languages, its economic structures and fragile sustainable environments, its creative solutions and resilience, as well as the combination of its pluralistic cultural-historical identity that still is a driving force in a global world. The authors invite colleagues to contribute to the enlargement of this research agenda. Thank you for your interest and attention to a few the of many Southern European challenges.

References

de Noronha T (2018) Mediterranean and migrations. *Journal of Mediterranean Knowledge* 3[1]

de Noronha T, Mangone E (2018) Historical contexts and identities of the mediterranean countries. *Journal of Spatial and Organizational Dynamics* 6[2]

European Commission (2016) Action Plan on the Integration of Third-Country Nationals. European commission, https://ec.europa.eu/home-affairs/sites/homeaffairs/files/what-we-do/policies/european-agenda-migration/proposal-implementation-package/docs/-20160607/communication_action_plan_integration_third-country_nationals_en.pdf

Vaz E, de Noronha T (2020) *Southern Europe – Major Trends and New Prospects*. Cities and Nature. Springer Verlag, London (forthcoming)

Articles

Volume 6, Number 1, 2019, 1–16
DOI: 10.18335/region.v6i1.208

journal homepage: region.ersa.org

Integrated local development in Mediterranean marginal territories: The case studies of Casentino (Italy), Algarve (Portugal) and Corse (France)

Andrea Ricci[1], Mario Biggeri[1,2], Andrea Ferrannini[1,3]

[1] ARCO (Action Research for CO-development), PIN Scrl, Prato, Italy
[2] University of Florence, Florence, Italy
[3] University of Ferrara, Ferrara, Italy

Received: 21 September 2017/Accepted: 17 October 2018

Abstract. Today, Mediterranean marginal territories are facing tremendous challenges. In the last decades, they have been characterised by a progressive abandonment in favour of urban areas, with consequent high social and environmental costs, such as the hydrogeological instability, degradation and soil erosion. However, at the same time they have relevant endogenous resources, which are often underutilized and unexploited and could be pivotal both for their strategic recovery, as well as for the economic and social development of the whole European Union.

This research investigates the potential active role of Mediterranean "marginal territories" to the achievement of the visions underlying the Europe 2020 strategy for smart, sustainable and inclusive growth. This paper aims to verify the idea that Mediterranean marginal and weak areas could lead their own development trajectories and, at the same time, actively contribute to harmonious development processes in Europe. The structure of this paper starts from general theoretical arguments and a short description of European policies for development. It follows with the diagnostic analysis of three territorial contexts selected as case-studies, i.e. Casentino (Italy), Algarve (Portugal) and Corse (France). Finally, it comes back to the general issues proposing implications and lessons learnt for the promotion of sustainable human development in Europe.

Key words: European and Mediterranean marginal territories, sustainable human development, territorial cohesion, Casentino, Algarve, Corse

1 Introduction

The importance of the relationship between territory and human development is undeniable in every historical phase, and in every place where human beings live. This relationship sees the territory as the dynamic and stratified result of a complex system of relations between living communities and the environment (Becattini 2014).

However, every development process creates territorial disequilibria and imbalances, with marginal territories often excluded from innovation processes and global knowledge networks due to their low competitiveness, capacities and accessibility. This marginality – especially in the case of inland and mountainous areas – often creates structural and long-term weaknesses, leading vicious cycles of abandonment and exclusion.

Marginal and weak territories in Europe, especially in mountainous and inland areas, have been historically characterised by a long and progressive abandonment in favour of urban areas, with consequent high social and environmental costs such as hydrogeological instability, degradation and soil erosion. The demographic decline coincides with the weakening of the supply of basic social services. In other words, "Europe is facing increasing and territorially differentiated challenges, and the risk of social exclusion is higher in areas with low accessibility, weak economic performance and lack of opportunities" (EU 2011, p. 5). Moreover, as clearly explained by Rodríguez-Pose (2018), persistent poverty, economic decay and lack of opportunities are at the root of considerable discontent in declining and lagging-behind areas, leading to the belief that these places have "no future" and "don't matter".

These marginal and weak territories are thus facing tremendous challenges, but at the same time they offer important potential for human development (UNDP 1990, Sen 1999) that must be exploited in order to find new trajectories for the human flourishing in Europe. Indeed, these areas are endowed with relevant endogenous resources – i.e. social, human and natural capital – that are often underutilized and unexploited, but could be pivotal both for their strategic recovery, as well as for the economic and social development of the whole European Union. Therefore, finding appropriate development trajectories for such areas could generate important benefits for a more harmonious development in Europe, strengthening cohesion and sustainability in economic, social and environmental terms. However, this could happen only if territories are able to propose ideas, models or development processes that are in relation to those of core areas and thus with other local development systems, in a necessary and mutual exchange of ideas, competences and services. In other words, if better policies are implemented focusing on tapping into untapped potential and on providing opportunities to those people living in the places that "don't matter" (Rodríguez-Pose 2018, p. 189).

The research hypothesis underlying this paper is that, in a reality dominated by global markets and territorial disequilibria, local systems in marginal territories still have, at least in the European context, the potentialities to take actively part at development processes, and not simply to survive in the global competitive environment. This perspective could be useful also to assess the effectiveness of multi-level relations between supranational policies (i.e. Agenda 2030, Europe 2020 with its Territorial Agenda and Cohesion Policy, etc.), national strategies and local development processes. In this regard, the Territorial Agenda of the European Union 2020 opened an important debate on the territorial dimension of policies and strategies. This Agenda provides a strategic orientation for territorial development and considers the Europe 2020 goals achievable only if the territorial dimension of the strategy is taken into account, arguing that "the diversity of territories is a potential for development and that the distinctive identities of local and regional communities are of key relevance in this regard" (EU 2011, p. 4).

Nowadays, it is therefore critically important to sustain renewed momentum around the long-term structural shifts required to meet the goal of the Europe 2020 strategy and the Agenda 2030 for Sustainable Development, especially in territories with marginal and peripheral characteristics, such as inland and mountainous areas.

The general objective of this paper is to investigate the potential active role of "marginal territories" to the achievement of the visions underlying the Europe 2020 strategy for smart, sustainable and inclusive growth. After this introduction, the paper is structured as follows. The second part is dedicated to a literature review on the relation between territories and human development and on the theoretical, interpretative framework on sustainable human development at local level. The third part contextualises the European policy framework for development in marginal and disadvantaged areas, while the fourth part describes the research design and the methodology used for data collection and analysis. The fifth part presents the results of the diagnostic analysis of three local development systems selected as case-studies due to their features of marginality and structural weaknesses: Casentino (Italy), Algarve (Portugal) and Corse (France). Based on this analysis, the sixth part highlights specific strategic actions to overcome the condition of marginality and to pursue sustainable human development trajectories. The last part summarises the final remarks and future perspectives.

2   The relationship between territory and human development

The relationship between territory and human development is at the centre of the theoretical framework underlying this paper. Among many, we consider Raffestin's definition of human territoriality as the more adequate for our purposes: "a complex system of relationships linking individuals or/and social groups with territory (exteriority) and with others (alterity) by means of mediators (instruments, techniques, representations etc.), in order to guarantee a maximum of autonomy within the limits of the system" (Raffestin 1980). Thus, Raffestin argues that the territory is generated starting from the relation between society and space, as actors "territorise" space.

In the last decades, concepts like "local development systems", "endogenous potential" and "local public goods" have acquired a central place in the academic literature due to the debate in economic geography and regional studies. According to Amin (1999), the idea at the base of local development is "to unlock the "Wealth of regions" as the prime source of development and renewal [...] in tending to favour bottom up, region specific, longer term and plural-actor based policy action" (Amin 1999, p. 368). In line with this reasoning, Pike et al. (2007, p. 1263) define development as the "establishment of conditions and institutions that foster the realization of the potential of the capacities and faculties of the human mind in people, communities and, in turn, places". This underlines also the territorial and people-centred perspective on Sustainable Human Development advanced by Biggeri, Ferrannini (2014), based on the recognition that the territory where individuals live and interact has fundamental importance for expanding or reducing economic and social capabilities, agency and empowerment. Therefore, these authors define Sustainable Human Development (SHD) at the local level as "a process of enabling the local system to function in order to facilitate the expansion of the real freedoms that people enjoy in an integrated and sustainable manner" (Biggeri, Ferrannini 2014, p. 147).

Moreover, the place-based approach to development strategies (Bolton 1992, Barca 2009) gives emphasis to the territorial context (in social, cultural and institutional terms),to multi-stakeholder and the interactive construction of knowledge in order to reinforce community capabilities and promote innovative ideas for the design of public policies and the tailored provision of public goods. In line with this argument, it is necessary to make development interventions more "place-aware" or "place-sensitive" by "taking into consideration the sheer variety of factors in diverse geographical location which may affect the potential returns of intervention" (Barca et al. 2012, p. 136). Nonetheless, the development of local systems is often based, through links between sectors and territories, on initiatives and actions taken in other places or by external institutions/agents (Becattini 2001). Therefore, it is crucial to recognise that local development does not simply depend on local efforts, but effective development trajectories can be pursued only if various levels are involved and aligned toward the achievement of common goals (Biggeri, Ferrannini 2014). In this regard, multilevel governance indicates the novel form of making public policy, due to the existence of "overarching, multilevel policy networks" (Marks 1996, p. 167), and could be understood as "a panoply of systems of coordination and negotiation, among formally independent but functionally interdependent entities" (Piattoni 2010, p. 26). The policy process must therefore be understood as an approach where local elites and endogenous actors interact with the external agents involved in the policies (Barca 2009). The importance of multi-level articulation lies in the ability to valorise endogenous resources by involving and including local stakeholders along with linking them with initiatives, resources and competences coming from other territories and higher governance levels. All in all, these arguments lead us to embrace an integrated approach for territorial diagnostics and analysis, taking into account, among others: socio-economic conditions; geography (density and accessibility); international global-local linkages; local, regional, national and communitarian policies for investment and innovation (Storper 1997, Pike et al. 2007, Crescenzi, Rodríguez-Pose 2011). The most innovative feature of this approach is thus the call for an integration of different levels of analysis, which have been historically separated and not treated with a systemic approach in a unique framework (Rodríguez-Pose, Crescenzi 2008), e.g. macro and micro economic theories with meso-level or regional ones; quantitative and qualitative analyses; top-down and bottom-up policy approaches. In particular, reconciling top-down and bottom-up development policies is necessary and critical to effectively foster sustainable human development at local level (Biggeri, Ferrannini 2014).

This integrated approach is appropriate to analyse the object of this paper – i.e. marginal and weak territories – and their endogenous potential. In theoretical terms, the idea of marginality is directly linked to the centre/periphery relation and to the issues of accessibility due to geographical, infrastructural, social and cultural factors. Marginality is mostly measured through simple quantitative parameters, such as the distance from agglomeration centres, often used in socioeconomic research on mountainous and inland areas.

The concepts of geographical and socio-economic marginality are also often correlated with the different types of weaknesses that may characterize a territory: e.g. weak as a consequence of human abandonment dynamics; weak as a consequence of absence of primary resources, services and capacities; weak in the sense of isolated, little, unknown and forgotten. These issues often require more complex quantitative-qualitative parameters that gravitate around the central elements of endowments, governance and capacities, as it will be discussed in the analysis of our case-studies.

3   European development policies for marginal territories

A large part of the European territory is characterised by the aggregation of citizens in minor centres, with limited accessibility to essential services. Since the War World II, the inland areas have been gradually and progressively subject to a process of marginalization characterised by demographic decrease, weakening of the supply of local basic services, high social cost for the whole country such as the hydrogeological instability and the environmental and cultural degradation (Dematteis 2013). In other words, as stated by Rodríguez-Pose (2018, p. 205), "years of decline, lack of opportunities and perceived neglect have put lagging-behind and declining areas in a state of flux".

For this reason, it is important to briefly recap the main development policies and instruments for marginal areas implemented by the EU with clear territorial objectives implications (in particular, the Cohesion Policy), in order to detect the evolution of the territorial dimension along with the integration process.

To begin with, it should be noted here that the Common Agricultural Policy and the Cohesion Policy are conceived to be the main EU "development instruments", allowing to better focus on specific objectives and making more efficient the sectorial policies through integrated actions, in line with the European Treaties (Rome, 1957; Maastricht, 1992; Amsterdam, 1997; Nice, 2001; Lisbon, 2007) and with the most recent Europe 2020 Strategy (see Table 1). Indeed, cohesion and convergence of the less developed areas have been regarded as a precondition for the competitiveness of the European Union as a whole.

Central attention needs to be paid to the EU Cohesion Policy as well as to the EU Rural Development Policy, as they both aim at promoting wellbeing and socio-economic stability for all the communitarian citizens, by investing on people and territories. Moreover, both policies are built on a multi-level governance mechanism (see Table 2) and on the participation of all the involved actors in development processes.

It is also important to briefly recap the evolution of the EU Cohesion Policy over the years. Indeed, the Cohesion Policy remains the main investment policy of the European Union and it is also the main policy tool to quickly answer to important crisis situations, directing funds where are more needed, and to sectors with high employability and growth rates.

Since the Rome Treaty of 1957, one of the main tasks of the Community has been to promote a "harmonious development of economic activities", by aiming "at reducing the disparities between the levels of development of the various regions" (Treaty of Rome, 1957). The need for a coordinated Community solution to regional imbalances was also recognized in the 1965 First Communication on Regional Policy. Thus, the idea of structuring aid for deprived regions started taking shape in the late 1960s, with the

Table 1: The Europe 2020 Strategy: Axes and Targets

Priorities Axes	Main Targets

a Smart growth: developing an economy based on knowledge and innovation through more effective investment in education, research and innovation;
 	
b Sustainable growth: promoting a more resource efficient, greener and more competitive economy decoupling economic growth from resource use thanks to a decisive move towards a low-carbon economy;
 	
c Inclusive growth: fostering a high-employment economy delivering social and territorial cohesion with a strong emphasis on job creation and poverty reduction.
	1. Employment: 75% of the 20-64 year-olds to be employed;
	
	2. R&D: 3% of the EU's GDP to be invested in Research and Development activities;
	
	3. Climate change and emission sustainability "20/20/20":
	
	  a Greenhouse gas emissions 20% lower than in 1990;
	
	  b 20% of energies from renewables.
	
	  c 20% increase in energy efficiency.
	
	4. Education:
	
	  i Reducing the rates of early school leaving below 10%;
	
	  ii At least 40% of the 30-34-year-olds completing the third level education;
	
	5. Fighting poverty and social exclusion: at least 20 million fewer people in or at-risk poverty and social exclusion.

Source: EC (2010)

Table 2: Multi-level Governance of the Planning Cycle 2014-2020

Communitarian Level	
STRATEGIC COMMON FRAMEWORK	
National Level	
Partnership Agreement (PA) & National Operative Programme (PON)	
Regional Level	
Regional Operative Programmes (POR) & Rural Development Programmes (PSR)	

Source: Author's elaboration

creation of the Directorate General for Regional Policy, which considered the support to underdeveloped regions "as important as the heart in the human body" and able to reanimate human life in the areas which have been denied it (Jean Rey, speech at the Directorate General for Regional Policy, 1968).

In 1971, the Council Resolution gave a strong incentive to regional development in Common Agricultural Policy (CAP) pursuing a policy of co-ordination of financial aids. After the "Thompson Report" and the enlargement of 1973, the European Regional Development Fund (ERDF) was set up for a 3-year test period, with the aim to correct regional imbalances.

At the beginning, the operations were purely national, and Member States had to apply for ERDF support at project level, while decisions were then taken in a committee of Member States based on Commission proposals. However, events such as the Single European Act, the Accession of Greece, Spain and Portugal, and the adoption of single market programmes gave a new impetus for a more genuine "European" Cohesion Policy. Indeed, these changes pushed new countries to increase regional disparities-funding as key means of bringing wealth up to EU average and set the basis for the overall framework underlying the Cohesion Policy designed to offset the burden of the single market for the less-favoured regions of the European Community.

In the 1988 for the first time the European Council allocate ECU 64 billion to Struc-

Table 3: Complementarity and integration between funds in 2014-2020 planning

European Structural and Investment Funds (ESI Funds: EFRD, ESF, CF, EAFRD, EMFF) to sustain the Cohesion Policy (reg. n. 1303/2013 note 2)		
Cohesion Policy (reg. EU n. 1303/2013)	Rural Development Policy (reg. EU n. 1306/2013)	Maritime and Fisheries Policy (reg. EU n. 508/2014)
European Regional Development Fund (ERDF), European Social Fund (ESF), Cohesion Fund (CF)	European Agriculture Fund for Rural Development (EAFRD)	European Maritime and Fisheries Funds (EMFF)

Source: Author's Elaboration on European Commission

tural Funds over 5 years, introducing the following four key principles: i) "concentration" (focusing on poorest regions), ii) "partnership" (involvement of regional and local partners), iii) "programming" (multiannual programming), and iv) "additionality" (of EU expenditure to national ones). This major shift from annual project selection by Member States to a more strategic and multi-annual programming conduced to a wider partnership between regions, Member States and the European Commission and toward a deeper integration of the structural funds around defined priority objectives.

The 1990s saw the standardization of rules, codification of principles of decentralized management and the increase of the structural fund budget from 16% to nearly 31% of EU budget. The budget reached ECU 168 billion over 5 years for Structural and Cohesion Funds according to the 1992 EU Treaty.

In the first years of the new millennium, the principle of "efficiency" was introduced to simplify design and procedures, putting the base for the enlargement of May 2004, when ten new Member States joined the Union. The 'Agenda 2000' paved the way for this historic enlargement that brought 20% increase in the EU population, but only 5% increase in GDP (EC 2010).

Within the programming cycle 2000-2006, around € 195 billion for the 3 Structural Funds and € 18 billion for the Cohesion Funds were budgeted together with other pre-accession instruments for capacity building, rural development, environmental protection and mobility (reg. EU n. 1303/2013). Moreover, the introduction of pre-accession instruments for candidates (ISPA) increased the structural fund budget to € 38 billion per year, reaching about 33% of EU budget.

For the planning period 2007-2013, the budget increased to about 36% of the total EU budget, focusing specifically on a growth and jobs strategy but still leaving rural development and fisheries funds outside cohesion policy.

Finally, the planning cycle 2014-2020 not only has been devoting funds for regional and cohesion policy amounting to € 351.8 billion, but it has also introduced an important innovation to favour the integration process, the complementarity and coherence among and within programmes: a unique regulation that sanction general dispositions on the functioning of all the funds (reg. EU n. 1303/2013), and that establish a unique body of funds shared by more policies (the ESI Funds) to implement Unitarian programmes and to align all communitarian policies with the goals of the Europe 2020 strategy (EC 2013).

Nonetheless, it is not easy – especially in places with lower institutional capacities – to be oriented in the complex functioning mechanism of European policies, which are composed by a multitude of strategies, regulations, priorities, funds, and intervention areas. The solution must be found in the complementarity among policies and funds: in the process of local integrated development the complementary has to become a concrete concept, especially when projects and programs are financed by more funds and impact on several local stakeholders.

In other words, better policies (from planning to implementation and evaluation) are needed in weak and marginal territories, described by Rodríguez-Pose (2018, p. 206) as follows: "Policies aimed at maximising the development potential of each territory, solidly grounded in theory and evidence, combining people-based with place-based approaches, and empowering local stakeholders to take greater control of their future". This vision is clearly aligned with the perspective of Sustainable Human Development at local level underlying this paper, which has been so far made operational only to a limited extent within the EU Cohesion Policy.

4   Research design and methodology

In order to answer the research question underlying this paper, a comparative case-study approach was adopted, by analysing the local development systems of Casentino valley in Tuscany (Italy), Algarve (Portugal) and Corse (France). These case-studies were selected as illustrative examples of marginal and weak territories in Southern Europe – the area with wider regional imbalances within the EU – in geographical and socio-economic terms. Obviously, it should be clarified that findings and arguments derived from this case-study approach can be extended to other similar areas in Europe only to a limited extent, without anyway limiting the relevance of this analysis.

The methodology was based on a harmonic range of different methods, which undoubtedly allowed to diversify the sources of information, digging deeper in all relevant topics and cross-checking findings and results, in order to obtain a comprehensive and consistent picture of the main issues in all areas. The high level of flexibility of the selected method was crucial to tailor them to the relevant target (e.g. different interviewees or group participants), making the whole methodology fully adaptable to the case-studies.

The methodology was mainly characterized by participatory observation and data collection, along with continuous informal and formal interaction with the community and with the main social, economic and political actors. The collection of qualitative data and information was developed in order to let emerge the voice, experiences and "reasons of actions" of all local stakeholders involved in the research. This was also supported by the analysis of secondary data, desk research and literature review in the fields of interest for the inquiry, and in some case by quantitative analysis to support and validate the findings of the qualitative information.

In particular, around 20 face-to-face semi-structured interviews and 4 focus group discusssions were conducted in each area as main data collection methods for our diagnostic analysis of the local development systems. The major goal of the interviews and focus group discussions was to generate a qualitative description to understand the weaknesses and the potentials of the local systems and to identify possible recovery strategy, concrete actions and projects to boost growth and employment in line with the Europe 2020 strategy. While semi-structured interviews had the crucial added-value of allowing to discuss multiple topics, with a certain freedom for the interviewee and interviewer, focus group discussions represented crucial occasions for participatory collective brainstorming to discuss relevant needs and potential solutions. Indeed, focus group discussions allowed the generation of strategic proposals working in interaction and collaboration with specific groups of stakeholders for each chosen territory, by leading participants to share opinions and impressions about the phenomena of interest and by stimulating the production of new ideas and creative proposals.

To conclude, the research followed a process articulated in multiple stages. In general, the procedure included i) identification of place-specific problems / opportunities deserving attention, ii) in-depth understanding of such weaknesses / potentials, iii) discussion of feasible scenarios to overcome such problems and to valorise the endogenous potentials, and iv) extrapolation of useful policy implications for marginal territories in general. In particular, the following steps (with their timing) were followed:

1. Literature review and desk research (02/2014 - 06/2017);

2. Research in Algarve (Portugal): territorial diagnostics, report and results validation (02/2014 – 06/2014);

3. Research in Casentino (Italy): territorial diagnostics, report and results validation (12/2014 – 08/2015);

4. Research in Corse (France): territorial diagnostics, report and results validation (04/2016 – 09/2016);

5. Compartive analysis (09/2016 – 05/2017).

Table 4: Synthetic data on Algarve, Casentino and Corse

	Algarve♣	Casentino♡	Corse◇
Administrative level	NUTS II	Sub-NUTS III	NUTS II
Main City	Faro	Bibbiena	Ajaccio
Main City Inhabitants - 2012	62,281	12,291	66,245
Area (km2)	4,995	700	8,680
Population - 2012	444,398	36,009	324,212
Density - 2012 (Inh./km2)	88.9	51.4	37.4
Foreign residents - 2012	14.1%	11.7%	9.1%
Old-age dependency ratio = 2012	30,7	27,9	26,1
GDP per capita - 2012 (€)	16,774	17,372	18,730
Unemployment rate - 2012	17.9%	18.8%	10.3%
No. of active firms - 2012	58,333	3,504	46,368
No. of incoming tourists - 2012	3,043,920	35,268	7,480,800

Source: ♣: INE (2013) and CCDR Algarve (2013); ♡: ISTAT (2012); ◇: INSEE (2014, 2015)

5   Diagnostic analysis of Local Development Systems

This chapter briefly presents the results of the territorial diagnostic analysis of the local development systems of Algarve, Casentino and Corse conducted through participatory methods during the field research. The diagnostics have been developed around four main dimensions:

- *Habitat* (i.e. natural environment and resources, anthropomorphic environment, infrastructural capital and intra/extra local mobility);

- *Community & Ethos* (i.e. local and extra-local socio-demographic dynamics, characteristics and trends, local identity, traditions, collective memory, material and immaterial cultural resources, civic participation and involvement in the decision-making processes);

- *Business* (i.e. economic and productive structures, sectorial analyses, occupational needs and employment opportunities);

- *Tourism* (i.e. endogenous vision, strengths, weaknesses, opportunities, threats, territorial capitals, quantitative analysis of fluxes, project proposals).

For the sake of synthesis, this chapter only presents an integrated assessment of the local development systems, by identifying strategic and critical intervention areas based on the SWOT (Strengths, Weaknesses, Opportunities and Threats) analysis for each territory.

5.1 Case-study 1: Algarve

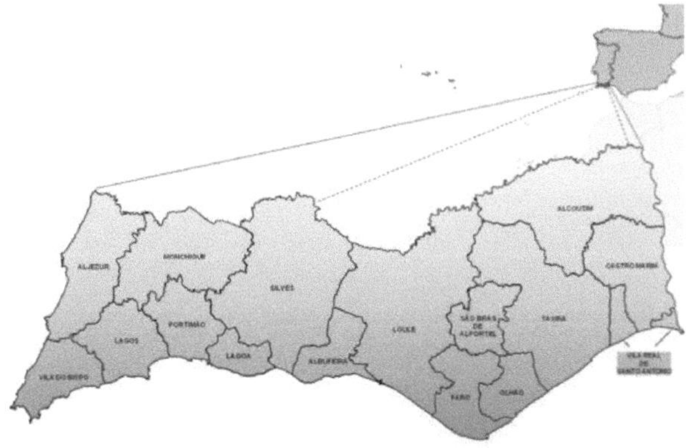

Source: CCDR Algarve (2007)

Figure 1: Algarve in Portugal and Europe

Table 5: Simplified SWOT analysis of Algarve

Strengths	Weaknesses
• Quality and variety of natural resources; • Airports with international flights and low-cost companies; • Quality, variety, competitiveness, reputation and consolidation of the touristic sector; • Other sectors with potential based on resources, existing know-how, in infrastructure and economic dynamics around tourism (e.g. sea, agro-industries, ICT, health or renewable energy). • High entrepreneurial rate with good spin-off capacity; • Favourable soil and climate conditions for agricultural activities.	• Atomization and overspecialization on the touristic sector in decline, and high levels of seasonality; • Levels of unemployment above the national average, accentuated by the negative performance of key regional economic activities; • Bad transportation system; • Deficits of leadership and training (individual and collective) and of coordination / cooperation of diverse nature, to enhance critical competitive, critic • mass and to empower the approach to other dimension markets. • Difficult to attract FDI and high-skilled workers.
Opportunities	**Threats**
• Promote diversification and enhancement of the regional economy (including tourism), leveraging other economic activities focused on market niche with high value / potentiality, taking advantage of the dynamics of tourism, of local resources, of available knowledge and capacity; • Promote the re-industrialization associated with the traditional sectors of the regional economy, boosting employment, generating value added and boosting cooperation networks / knowledge transfer between research centres and the business world.	• Inability to boost diversification and valorisation of local potentialities; • Loss of competitiveness and international attractiveness of the Algarve, as a tourist destination or as destinations of investment; • Inability to boost cooperation networks especially focused on the use of the economic potentials of the region (e.g. networks of cooperation companies, regional innovation system); • Slow implementation of new energetic sources in the region.

Source: Author's elaboration

5.2 Case-study 2: Casentino

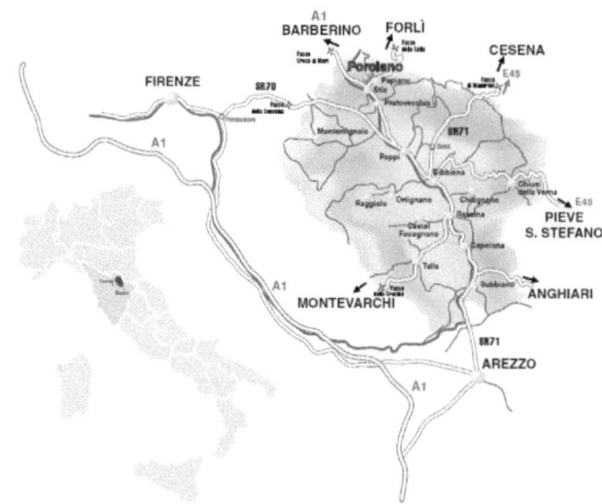

Source: http://www.castellodiporciano.com

Figure 2: Casentino in Tuscany and Italy

Table 6: Simplified SWOT analysis of Casentino

Strengths	Weaknesses
• Natural integrity and wonderful landscapes: important quantity and quality of natural resources and high quality of life;	• Insufficient mobility system with the population facing barriers to use it (critical situation for nonmotorized mobility);
• Good social capital, high level of social trust, and positive reciprocities' system;	• Very marked ageing dynamic and negative natural growth rate of the population, youth emigration;
• Ancient craftsmanship knowledge (wood, stone, iron and wool);	• Very weak and fragmented governance systems;
• Strong identity and sense of belonging;	• Reduction of important historical production chains (textile, wood, agro-forestry-pastoral)
• High entrepreneurial rate with good spin-off capacity and high diversification of the economic activity;	• Difficulties to attract high-skilled workers and FDI;
• Emergence of new enterprises in ICTs and high value-added sectors and presence of leader companies.	• Relative isolation of the area, scarce accessibility and lack of telematics networks, scarce services' supply.
Opportunities	**Threats**
• Develop effective "feeder system" for public transportation (demand responsive or dial-a-ride public TS), empower the non-motorized mobility system;	• Hydrogeological risk and instability (eco-systemic disequilibria);
• Exploit the opportunities for social and environmental development / protection through coordination (fund rising) and mutual knowledge (efficiency) among associations;	• Closeness to the outside world could generate exclusion phenomena, tensions and conflicts;
	• Progressively ageing population, higher incidence of social and productive problems;
• Activate synergies and collaborations between different sectors (agro-food-tourism);	• Emigration of younger generations and difficulties in inter-generational passages;
• Promote the tourism sector and the proximity with important touristic destinations (Florence, Siena, Rome etc.).	• The economic crisis and the bankrupt of important enterprises and territorial banks: risk of financial and economic contagion and troubles.

Source: Author's elaboration

5.3   Case-study 3: Corse

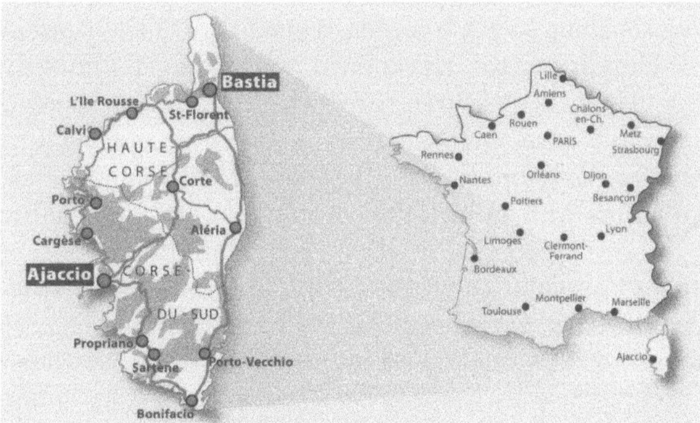

Source: http://www.mapsman.com

Figure 3: Corse in France

Table 7: Simplified SWOT analysis of Corse

Strengths	Weaknesses
• Quality and variety of natural resources, wonderful landscapes, high quality of life;	• Bad transportation system;
• Diffused cultural, architectonical and natural heritage;	• Progressively ageing population, higher incidence of social and productive problems;
• Quality, variety, competitiveness, reputation and consolidation of the touristic sector;	• Reduction of important historical production chains (tannin, wood, agro-forestry-pastoral)
• Undiscovered, unexplored and secret place different from the national context (speculated in the collective imaginary, and in touristic marketing);	• Levels of unemployment above the national average;
• Strong identity and sense of belonging;	• Very marked ageing dynamic of the population, negative natural growth rate of the population and youth emigration create difficulties in the intergenerational turnover, and weaken the local community;
• Consolidated market in primary sector;	
• Persistence of cultural traditions and craftsmanship knowledge;	• Small Enterprises highly dependent on the national market and with scarce entrepreneurial culture.
• Airports with international flights and low-cost companies.	
Opportunities	**Threats**
• Empower non-motorized mobility system and develop effective "feeder system" for public transportation;	• Hydrogeological risk and instability;
• Activate synergy and collaboration between different sectors to generate important economies of scale and scope (agro-food-tourism);	• Slow implementation of new energetic sources in the region;
	• Insane forest expansion as consequence of agropastoral activities reduction;
• Create integrated local production chains (agro-food-tourism);	• Resistance to changes by older generation, and little openness to innovation;
• Opportunity for the de-seasonality of the touristic demand (snow, ski, chestnuts, etc.) and to create attractive touristic packages in all seasons.	• Losses of knowledge and know-how in important sectors (wood, textile) and disappearance of important artisanal activities (wood, stone, iron, wool);
	• Progressively ageing population, higher incidence of social/productive problems.

Source: Author's elaboration

5.4 Comparative findings

The population dynamics of these territories had been strongly negative till the 1980s, since then they have continued with a stable trajectory till the present day. It seems that, despite the losses of human capital, these local systems have found dynamic equilibriums.

The primary resource of these three territories is in their environmental, natural and cultural richness. Despite the huge amount of natural and cultural resources, people living in such territories face important problems and barriers to access essential services (e.g. education, health) as well as in terms of internal and external mobility.

Therefore, a primary precondition to tap into untapped potential and to provide wider socio-economic opportunities to the people living in those places is to increase the spatial accessibility and the services usability. In particular, to stop the abandonment dynamics of the local population and to create conditions for the younger generations to live and build their future in these areas, it is essential to enhance the quality and accessibility of basic services for the resident people, guaranteeing essential services such as high quality educational supply for the youths, adequate health care assistance, and create employment opportunities. In fact, one of the main economic weaknesses of these areas seems to be their infrastructural endowments. On the one hand, the low level of internal infrastructural development is undoubtedly a comparative disadvantage for many local businesses, which are penalised in term of transportation costs. This has also led to a relevant fragmentation and atomization of the entrepreneurial base in these areas, with limited economies of scale and learning. On the other hand, this low level of infrastructural endowment may have created a competitive advantage in terms of territorial / landscape distinction with respect to the regional and national contexts, having also limited the diffusion of external (and often cheaper) products.

Moreover, the above-mentioned economic fragmentation is also reflected at institutional and governance levels, with a wide number of public entities having diversified (and sometimes overlapping) responsibilities in decision-making, policy design and public administration.

Finally, these areas share the potential for strategies based on their attractiveness in terms of sustainable tourism destinations and on the quality of their agro-food production, being both characterised by elements of cultural tradition, integrity and respect for the environment.

6 Policy implications for Mediterranean marginal territories

The diagnostic analysis of Casentino, Algarve and Corse local development systems, which could be taken as reference territories for other similar areas in Europe, together with the analysis of the European policy framework for marginal areas stimulates a reflection on the marginal conditions of such territories leading to a more general overview of the possible development trajectories, scenarios and conditions that could be applied in other territorial contexts.

The territory is not an enterprise, thus, it cannot close for bankruptcy. It could be depopulated of people and activities, but the territory cannot close and die. Therefore, a place-based and people-centred approach to territorial development makes sense only in a policy framework open to the evolution and integration of multiple models, strategies, and development trajectories.

In order to foster their development processes, it is primarily necessary to reduce the marginality through accessibility: basic services (education and health care), spatial and virtual accessibility. Accessibility means to allow person to live, host, travel, build social relations, develop businesses and create jobs and wealth. Therefore, in order to create the conditions for a real contribution of such areas to the overall development of the European Union, it is necessary to implement strategies to protect and enjoy their citizenship rights, and to sustain the local (and thus national and European) economic growth starting from their untapped endogenous potential.

According to the previous analysis and considerations, a crucial condition to overcome the territorial weakness of many European local development systems is to "open" the local context itself.

The openness of marginal territory could be conceived as:

- Openness to external resources: financial resources (e.g. European Funds) and innovation leverages, such as universities or R&D centres (Noronha Vaz, Cesário 2005);

- Institutional openness through the application of multilevel governance models among different administrative levels;

- Construction of inter-municipal, trans-regional and trans-national cooperation networks, which could assume different forms and allow good practice exchanges and formative experiences of territorial programming, management and development among local administrations, technicians and administrators;

- Openness to global markets through internet and technological innovations (Noronha Vaz, Cesário 2005).

Thus, the uniqueness of a territorial system has to be included in a broader set of trans-local network relations, however, this could weaken and threaten the same uniqueness that characterizes the local system. For instance, in many cases territorial development practices are focused on the valorisation of the historical-cultural-environmental heritage in touristic terms, placing much effort on tourism promotion and valorisation. However, often such interventions aim at homologating the local attractiveness around folkloristic images built on a presumed local identity, or around alternative emergent touristic segments (agro-tourism, cultural tourism, rural development, etc.).

Another condition concerns capacities and opportunities, in the sense of assimilation and application of the knowledge and skills that empower people to purse their aspirations, businesses to pursue their objectives, institutions to pursue local development and well-being. From this perspective it makes sense to think that a territory could acquire the functioning to express new, complementary and sustainable development models (Biggeri, Ferrannini 2014), offering its own contribution to the external world instead of being conceived as "places that don't matter". This broad capacity-building condition includes for instance:

- To promote knowledge and know-how production, diffusion and reproduction, starting from local embedded knowledge, and encouraging and investing in research and development activities aiming at finding new and innovative way to foster socio-economic development;

- Construction of socio-economic and productive networks, in the sense of industrial districts and clusters (Becattini et al. 2009) based on cooperation-competition mechanisms among local SMEs and other local stakeholders.

The acquisition of planning, operative, cooperative and governance capacities at the local level could contribute to change the defining parameters of territorial marginality and weakness. In addition to structural socio-economic factors, they give importance to the capacity to react to top-down stimulus and promoting their own strategic and enlarged development vision.

In addition, another condition is the enhancement of social capital and trust in the possibility to act in a situation of scarce resources. It is necessary to believe and stimulate the changing of the local entrepreneurs and administrators' behaviours in order to jointly exploit economies of learning and scope for the local system. In this regard, it appears relevant to:

- Enhance the governance system and its administrative processes, through the improvement of the social dialogue, the capacity to elaborate, collaborate, share, and co-act, posing a primary goal for collective wellbeing, but recognizing the interdependence of individual development trajectories (Sen 2009).

- Sustain the valorisation of endogenous territorial and cultural capital, as the local identity has a dynamic value with respect to history, traditions, and knowledge. Therefore, it is necessary to activate participatory processes able to trigger the sense of belonging for a development path (Biggeri, Ferrannini 2014, Biggeri et al. 2018).

Finally, as we have seen, the core of the current communitarian policies is the promotion of smart, inclusive and sustainable growth, which makes reference to a unique development framework where cohesion and sustainability are functional to these priorities.

In order to embrace the territorial dimension of policies, it is thus necessary to re-start from the territories, utilizing an operative and realistic approach, which could take into account the relevant issues, the priorities of development strategies and the various forms of internal and external collaboration and partnerships.

7 Final Remarks

The centrality and specificity of the territory and its resources has changed the view on local development paradigms: it is not yet acceptable to consider a unique direction where localities have to converge, at the same way, and it does not make sense to consider a universal model which represent a prototype of developed society; instead, there is a multiplicity of local models. The destiny of marginal areas is not to converge with developed ones, but to take their own unique irreproducible trajectory.

Nonetheless, local development and cohesion policies at national and European level have not been adequate in the last years to tackle the challenges they face. Many European territories are far from overcoming their own structural weaknesses and deficits to build the base for the flourishing of the endogenous potential. The affirmation of certain local development models and the valorisation of endogenous resources are very complex processes, which have to face the reality of challenges based on: the real potential of a territory, the real predisposition of local actors, the internal and external real demand, the extra-local programming context, and the global dynamics.

On these premises, marginal territories can (and should) play a fundamental role in ensuring equilibrium, cohesion and sustainability in the European development process. Although the territorial dimension in the process of European policies and scenarios is increasingly marked, this does not imply that marginal territories themselves are conscious to be part of such scenarios. It is clear that Europe is perceived, at the local context, mainly as a potential source of funds, but also as imposing constraints, recently leading to increased populism and anti-Europe feelings.

Therefore, analysing territorial unbalances from the perspective of marginal territories could be a way to check if there are intersections between communitarian scenarios and territorial realities. The European territorial development scenarios are defined by priorities and political choices that aim to react to the main global challenges, but it seems crucial to design development processes to be tailored on the territories and through the territories themselves. Specifically, marginal territories provide development issues, models and opportunities that deserve to be taken into account within European and national policy-making and instruments provision.

The potentials of marginal territories to contribute to harmonious development process within the EU may consist in a series of elements such as: the design and pursuit of their own local development trajectories; the construction of extra-local, trans-regional and trans-European networks; the operationalization of the development principles (sustainability, cohesion, polycentrism, competitiveness, etc.); the closeness to the needs and aspirations of citizens; the tailored adaption of extra-local strategies.

Moreover, the development processes and practices in marginal territories (which start from worse conditions) could allow territories and their actors to acquire a superior consciousness of their own active roles, to be able to directly contribute to the local, national and European development and to define new complementary forms of polycentrism with respect to the global ones. Thus, they can contribute developing their own conditions and becoming conscious to be part of an enlarged system, opening up to external resources, global markets, in institutional terms and in the construction of multilevel cooperation and socio-economic productive networks.

In other words, marginal territories could provide innovative people-centred and place-based conceptualizations and operationalizations of the core development ideas and models underlying the European Union. Although there is no guarantee that their contribution will be successful, this people-centred and place-based approach seems to offer the best option to enhance the capabilities of people and communities to flourish within a sustainable human development perspective.

References

Amin A (1999) An institutionalist perspective on regional economic development. *International Journal of Urban and Regional Research* 23[2]: 365–378. CrossRef.

Barca F (2009) An agenda for a reformed cohesion policy: A place-based approach to meeting European Union challenges and expectations. Independent report prepared at the request of the European Commissioner for regional policy, Danuta Hübner, European Commission, Brussels

Barca F, McCann P, Rodriguez-Pose A (2012) The case for regional development intervention: Place-based versus place-neutral approaches. *Journal of Regional Sciences* 52[1]: 134–152. CrossRef.

Becattini G (2001) Metafore e vecchi strumenti: Ovvero delle difficoltà d'introdurre il 'territorio' nell'analisi socio-economica. In: Becattini G, Bellandi M, Dei Ottati G, Sforzi F (eds), *Il Caleidoscopio dello sviluppo locale. Trasformazioni economiche nell'Italia contemporanea*. Rosenberg & Sellier, Turin

Becattini G (2014) Prologue. In: Biggeri M, Ferrannini A (eds), *Sustainable Human Development: A New Territorial and People-Centred Perspective*. Palgrave Macmillan, London

Becattini G, Bellandi M, De Propris L (2009) *A handbook of industrial districts*. Edward Elgar Publishing, Cheltenham. CrossRef.

Biggeri M, Ferrannini A (2014) *Sustainable Human Development: A New Territorial and People-Centred Perspective*. Palgrave Macmillan, Basingstoke and New York. CrossRef.

Biggeri M, Ferrannini A, Arciprete C (2018) Local communities and capability evolution: The core of human development processes. *Journal of Human Development and Capabilities* 19[2]: 126–146. CrossRef.

Bolton R (1992) 'place prosperity vs people prosperity' revisited: An old issue with a new angle. *Urban Studies* 29[2]: 185–203. CrossRef.

CCDR Algarve – Comissão de Coordenação e Desenvolvimento Regional do Algarve (2007) Plano Regional de Ordenamento do Território do Algarve – PROTAlgarve. Comissão de Coordenação e Desenvolvimento do Algarve, Faro

CCDR Algarve – Comissão de Coordenação e Desenvolvimento Regional do Algarve (2013) Algarve Preparar o Futuro, Diagnóstico Prospetivo 2014-2020. Comissão de Coordenação de Desenvolvimento Regional, Faro

Crescenzi R, Rodríguez-Pose A (2011) Reconciling top-down and bottom-up development policies. *Environment and Planning* 43[4]: 773–780

Dematteis G (2013) La montagna nella strategia per le aree interne 2014-2020. *Agriregionieuropa* 34

EC – European Commission (2010) Europe 2020: A strategy for smart, sustainable and inclusive growth. COM(2010) 2020 final, Brussels

EC – European Council (2013) Laying down the multiannual financial framework for the years 2014-2020. No 1311/2013 of 2 December 2013, OJ L 347, 20.12.2013, p. 884-891

EU – European Union (2011) Territorial agenda of the European Union 2020. Towards an inclusive, smart and sustainable Europe of diverse regions. agreed at the Informal Ministerial Meeting of Ministers responsible for Spatial Planning and Territorial Development on 19th May 2011 Gödöllö, Hungary

INE – Instituto Nacional de Estatística (2013) Anuário Estatístico da Região do Algarve 2012. Instituto Nacional de Estatística, Lisboa

INSEE – Institut National de la Statistique et des Etudes Economiques (2014) Annual national accounts. Institut National de la Statistique et des Etudes Economiques, Paris

INSEE – Institut National de la Statistique et des Etudes Economiques (2015) Gross domestic product (GDP) and main economic aggregates. Institut National de la Statistique et des Etudes Economiques, Paris

ISTAT – Istituto Statistico Nazionale (2012) 15 censimento della popolazione e delle abitazioni, struttura demografica e familiare della popolazione residente. Istituto Statistico Nazionale, Roma

Marks G (1996) An actor-centred approach to multi-level governance. *Regional and Federal Studies* 6[2]: 20–40. CrossRef.

Noronha Vaz T, Cesário M (2005) Behavioural patterns towards innovation: the case of European rural regions. Proceedings of XVI ISPIM Conference: Porto, Portugal - The Role of Knowledge in Innovation Management - ISBN 952-214-059-7

Piattoni S (2010) *The Theory of Multi-Level Governance. Conceptual, Empirical, and Normative Challenges.* Oxford University Press, Oxford

Pike A, Rodríguez-Pose A, Tomaney J (2007) What kind of local and regional development and for whom? *Regional Studies* 41[9]: 1253–1269. CrossRef.

Raffestin C (1980) *Pour une géographie du pouvoir.* éd LITEC, Paris

Rodríguez-Pose A (2018) The revenge of the places that don't matter (and what to do about it). *Cambridge Journal of Regions, Economy and Society* 11[1]: 189–209. CrossRef.

Rodríguez-Pose A, Crescenzi R (2008) Mountains in a flat world: Why proximity still matters for the location of economic activity. *Cambridge Journal of Regions, Economy and Society* 37[1]: 1–18. CrossRef.

Sen AK (1999) *Development as Freedom.* Oxford University Press, Oxford. CrossRef.

Sen AK (2009) *The idea of justice.* Allen Lane, London

Storper M (1997) *The Regional World: Territorial Development in a Global Economy.* Guilford Press, New York

UNDP – United Nations Development Programme (1990) *Human Development Report 1990 - Concept and measurement of human development.* Oxford University Press, New York

Volume 5, Number 1, 2018, 113–137
DOI: 10.18335/region.v5i1.218

journal homepage: region.ersa.org

Rehabilitation and Renewal of Mediterranean Structures. The Utopic Landscape of Algarve

Carlos Bragança dos Santos[1]

[1] Universidade do Algarve, Faro, Portugal

Received: 29 September 2017/Accepted: 4 April 2018

Abstract. One of the remarkable features of Mediterranean landscapes is the terraced land frame, usually supported by dry stone walling. The terraces, property division walls, pathways and traditional paths design a network compartmentalization that defines landscape identity. The informational content, aesthetic quality, ecological and cultural values allowed by this articulated construction are particularly important at coastal zones with intense human impact. On the Algarve, the hills displayed by such structures form the backdrop of an urban-touristic system. This paper aims to interrelate ecological, aesthetic, symbolic, socio-economic and political aspects that influence the spatial distribution and image of the terraces. The values that local people may assign to their landscapes will determine the acknowledgement of the structural elements under analysis, but the role of tourists must be seriously take into account. Beyond nostalgic solutions, one must prospect the future of the dry stone walling structure into the diversity of possible solutions for a sustainable landscape development, which enhances the living part of an inseparable unit that includes the densest urbanized areas with less ecological functions. We call such a unit the urban-touristic region of Algarve and, therefore, we try to use landscape as an instrument of knowledge and acknowledgement of regional spaces.

JEL classification: Q56

Key words: Terraces, Landscape, Urban-Region, Mediterranean, Algarve

1 Introduction

In the Mediterranean context, the landscape is the outcome of a very long building process. "Landscapes are never completed. Rather, they are constantly being built and rebuilt through people's engagement with their inner images and with their physical environment." (Backhaus et al. 2008).

In order to understand the dynamics of a complex system such as the landscape, under a systemic approach, the first thing to do is to combine its structural aspects to reach a model of the system's functioning. However, in the case of landscape, we need to surpass the mechanist trends on approaching the biophysical and aesthetic features as merely observable and measurable objects, as if they were outside of ourselves. Thus, we will try to get closer to a mesological meaning of the landscape –landscape as a mediatory function between people and the environment (Berque 1986).

Under this perspective, in addition to the relationship with other structural elements of different dimensions, cultural, ecological, sociopolitical, economic and spiritual, a structural feature of landscape can never be outside of individuals, as human subjects and, most of all, as a society. Therefore, the involvement of all relevant dimensions underlie the way we will seek to frame the analysis of dry stone walling structure at the barrocal[1] of the Algarve region. In fact, we focus on a very representative structure modeling of the mountains and hills that fit the skeleton of many Mediterranean landscapes (Braudel 2001).

We begin with a short description of the main features of Mediterranean environment, as a distinctive broad region, in both biophysical and socio-cultural terms, in which the Algarve is included. The role of dry stone structure on terraced landscapes as hard work done by many generations that carved a regional hallmark is a very important aspect. In that sense, some functions and building aspects of dry stone walling will appear as an explanation of accumulated knowledge. However, one can only reach the real significance and the future of such distinctive structures by emphasizing the construction of landscape as a process.

Indeed, it appears obvious that the prevailing ideas of the world guide the general process of landscape construction. One cannot detach the evolution of the landscape and the actions that transform the places, from the ideas and the strategic framework derived from beliefs, either religious or philosophical. For instance, the rapid landscape changes that we are witnessing nowadays, usually leading to well-known unsustainable territories with no apparent solution, are a consequence of a prevailing dualism inherited from the Aristotelian logic.

Such an absence of solutions compels us to display positive utopias to prospect the evolution of landscape as both a common good and a place with enough biological activity to withstand large urban concentration. Therefore, we explore the idea of an urban-tourist region at the Algarve as the scenario of the various activities most likely to influence the future of the landscape structure supported by dry stone walling. The focus on a regional approach to landscape counteracts the idea of landscapes as closed entities, eventually with an optimal condition or climax state (Backhaus 2011), thus allowing its complete control. Rather, we agree that landscape evolution must comprehend constant negotiations about possible trajectories. In that sense, we present a method as a platform to facilitate communication and encourage public participation, essential to legitimize real options.

In brief, our general methodology comprehends the following steps: 1) a short prospect of the geographical environment of the Algarve's terraced landscape, enhancing perceptual features, hidden aspects and the real tensions; 2) a general description of socio-cultural relationships of the terraced landscape, building techniques, main functions, limitations and threats; 3) a search for alternative strategies on landscape reconstruction as a process, thus suggesting the utopia of an Algarve urban region; and 4) an exploration of the four poles method for the interpretation of landscape. Our goal is to discuss and design a process of knowledge and acknowledgment of a structure that shapes the character of the 'Algarvian' landscape and not necessarily to present finished solutions.

2 Geographic Overview of the Algarve

The Algarve region is located in the Gulf of Cadiz, practically in the vestibule of the western entrance of the Mediterranean Sea, known as the Hercules Columns. Mediterranean influences are present, at the climate level, in the vegetation cover and even in people's traditions. Then, one can observe many characteristic features of Mediterranean landscapes, like the terraces of barrocal hills, a distinctive factor of Algarve's landscape.

---

[1]'Barrocal' could be understood like clay (barro, in Portuguese and Spanish) plus lime (cal, idem), meaning –in real physical terms– a fine layer of clay –mostly 10 to 20 cm of clay– over an extensive mass of lime rock. It is a zone where water infiltration is very important and leads to a progressive dissolution of limestone; a karstic process takes place, forming big aquifers with various depths, normally reaching hundreds of meters (Costa et al. 1985). Nevertheless, according to a famous dictionary of Portuguese language (Machado 1991), the term barrocal comes from barroco meaning an isolated big rock or a place full of big rocks.

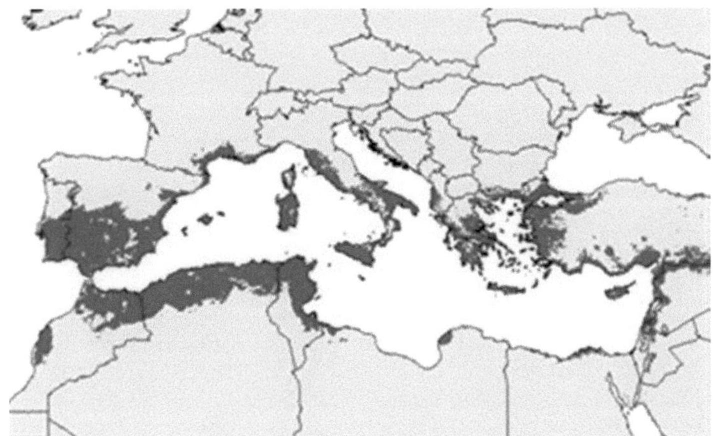

Source: Adapted from Oteros (2014)

Figure 1: Ecological niche of the potential olive tree distribution

These terraces, supported by dry stone walling structures built over generations, play a decisive role in the conservation of traditional agrosystems, not only as cultural and ecological values but also in aesthetic terms.

2.1 The Mediterranean context

The first issue to clarify is the integration of the Algarve in the Mediterranean geographical context. According to Forman (1995), the microclimate and the socio-cultural pattern are the two broad characteristics for defining a region. In fact, the Mediterranean climate extends a little beyond the shores of Mediterranean Sea, embracing at least the south of Iberian Peninsula. One could say that the Mediterranean region, extends until the doorway of Hercules Columns, "[the region] contrasts mightily with the Sahara area to the south, temperate Europe to the north, and a cool, dry region to the east. The Mediterranean Region is distinctive in both physical and human terms." (Forman 2008, p. 11). As the Portuguese geographer, Orlando Ribeiro used to say, the Mediterranean influence goes until the last olive tree (Figure 1).

Throughout the Mediterranean coastal regions, the omnipresence of mountains is very characteristic. "The Mediterranean space is devoured by mountains. They are present until the seafront, abusive, leaning against each other, inevitable, like the skeleton and the background of landscape." (Braudel 2001, p. 19).

It is true that the mountain ranges of the Algarve are not as visually impressive as in other Mediterranean coastal areas. The low elevation of the hills –less than 400 meters– and the progressive abandonment of traditional agricultural activities coarsen the perceptual field and the 'sense of mystery' can only be revealed when the beholder come closer. In fact, a façade of limestone hills, with an alignment roughly parallel to the coastline, is omnipresent as the backdrop of most urban concentrations. The geometric disposal of mountains shapes a sort of amphitheater opened to the sea. A second line of shale Mountains, the 'Serra', behind the limestone hills, reinforces the protection from the inconvenient cold north winds and makes the prevailing of meridional influences in all the littoral and part of the barrocal (Figure 2).

2.2 The backdrop and the 'skeleton' of the landscape

Despite the evident presence of a backdrop, the truth is that the strong urban growth along the coast created a considerable distance between people and their landscape, leading to several situations of loss of attractiveness and even degradation. However, under sustainable conditions, landscapes can tell their stories again in a way that people may

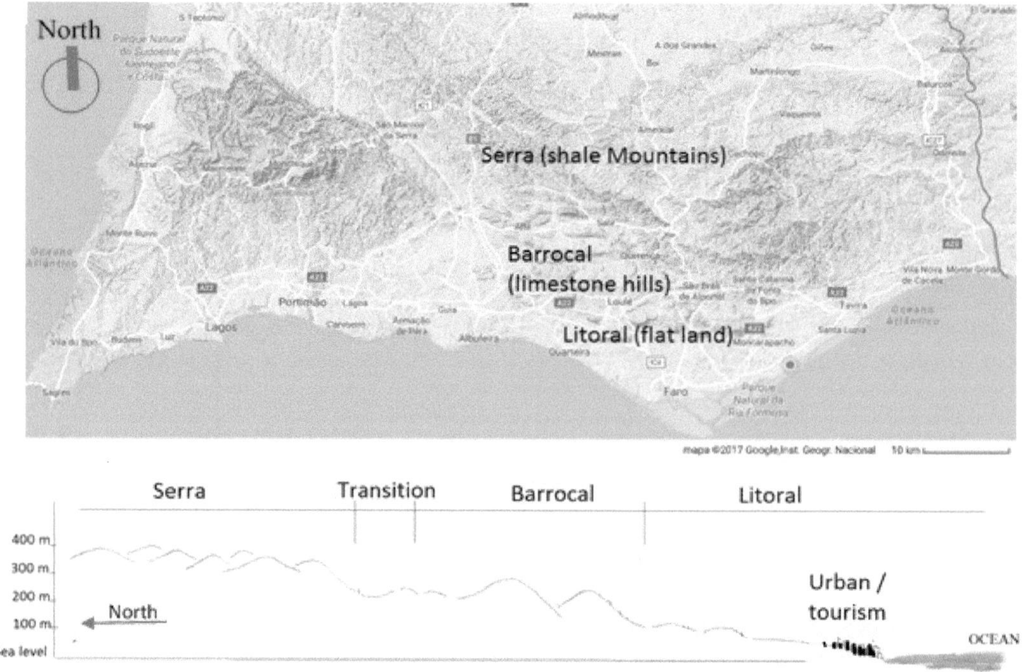

Figure 2: The different types of Algarve relief: Top: digital terrain model (adapted from google maps, 2017); Bottom: profile sketch from North to South

appreciate their narrative and poetic qualities[2] again (Nohl 2001). Once the perception of many hidden aspects is not evident, the consciousness of sustainable conditions is often difficult to achieve, especially for outside observers. For that reason we empathize some concerns about critical biophysical functions and intrinsic tensions.

In fact, the barrocal exactly matches that homogeneous zone in terms of soil (chalky) and climate features, formed by the hills mentioned before. Here prevails the unirrigated orchard agrosystem, developed on terraces that constitute the hallmark of the Algarve rural countryside (Feio 1983). Much of this zone is, in fact, the background of the landscape perceived from the urban-tourist concentration along the coastline, which was spreading from the 1970s, like in many Mediterranean coastal areas.

Given that the geological bedrock of the barrocal is mostly from the Jurassic period (Figure 3), then one must take into account that the limestone dissolution generates a complex set of aquifers interlinked in the underground (Costa et al. 1985). Most of these aquifers have a high productivity and good water quality; until nowadays they were poorly exploited and provided the urban water supply up to the end of the 1990s. Then, after the year 2000, a system of dams ensured urban water supply, thus increasing the risk of eutrophication, and underground water has become more intensively used for irrigated agriculture.

Moreover, this irrigated agriculture, developed just above the largest regional aquifer, matching the northern part of Jurassic bedrock, with obvious consequences for the degradation of groundwater quality, which was partially financed by EU funds (Bragança 2006). In addition to this vital negative impact, the massive incidence of dryland transformation in irrigated land lead to a gradual substitution of part of the traditional terraced landscape. On the other hand, when soil sealing large areas of the barrocal or extracting large quantities of underground water, some disturbances can happen in the control of the salt wedge, leading to soil salinization at the littoral zone (Figure 4).

Like in other Mediterranean coastal regions, especially where the limestone relief dominates, the hydro-geological protection is undoubtedly an issue of great importance

---

[2]Nohl (2001) points out two close related aspects for landscape aesthetics: 1) the narrative aspects, related to perceptions and symptoms about the landscape functioning; 2) the poetic aspects, related to mood/feelings and symbols/meanings.

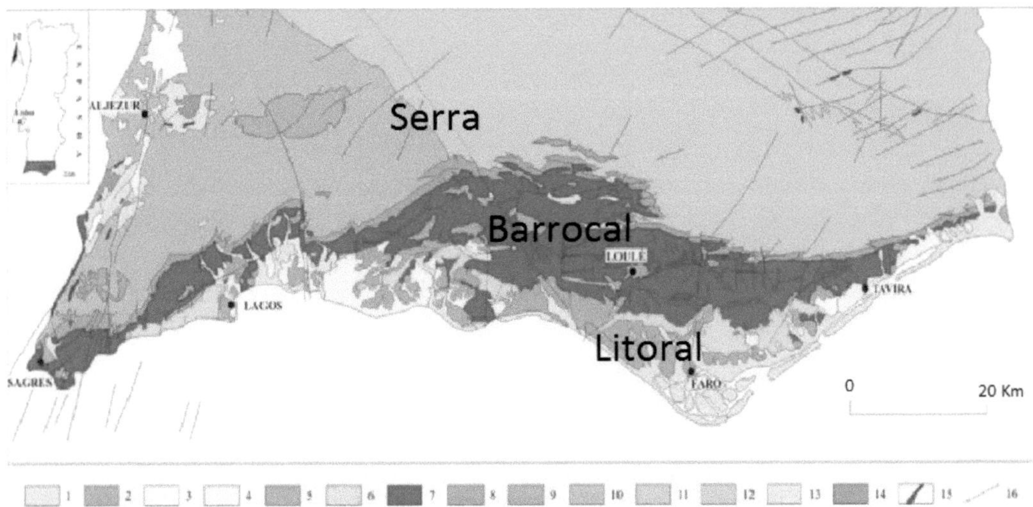

Source: Adapted from Carta Geológica de Portugal, scale 1:500 000, 1992
Notes: Typical cenozoic substratum of Litoral: 1 Holocene; 2 Pleistocene; 3 Pliocene; 4 Miocene; 5, Paleogene. Typical mesozoic substratum of Barrocal: 6 Cretaceous; 7 Jurassic. Transition Barrocal–Serra: 8 early Jurassic–Late Triassic. Substratum of Serra: 9 Igneous intrusive massive of Monchique: 10 Vestefalian, 11 Namurian, 12 Visean, 13, Tournaisian, 14 Famennian. Complementary information: 15 reefs, 16 faults.

Figure 3: Geological map of Algarve

(Fontanari 2008, Lasanta et al. 2013). Here, favoring infiltration, mitigating the effects of torrentiality and controlling the risk of erosion, improving soil quality, are significant considerations of such protection. All these features closely links with the spatial distribution and traditional building techniques using local materials. The materials that form the dry stone walling that supports the terraces platforms come from the work of taking some stones from the previously existing relief. The resulting dry stone walling assures an effective drainage of a greatest thickness of clay soil.

Urbanites and tourists hardly realize such features, as well as the historic-cultural background and the actual range of ecological functions fulfilled by the resulting traditional agrosystems. However, from an aesthetical standpoint, these land support walls, when combined with other property separation walls and paths limitation, define an extended constructive body, which design a kind of landscape calligraphy encompassing complex alignments and rhythms. One can easily perceive a compartmentation, which sustain the ecological diversity and defines the geometry of the entire space as well.

3 Traditional Building Structures

In fact, one must remember that Mediterranean landscape terraces are quite resilient. Throughout their history there were cycles with periods of building and expansion followed by stability and then declining periods with abandonment, before repeating a new cycle (Guerny, Hsu 2010). Moreover, evident social factors strengthened resilience, such as the nature of collective work and social organization needed for the construction process, but also the continuous surveillance and team organizations for quick repairs in case of great damages. On the other hand, these aspects cannot be isolated from traditional techniques.

3.1 Historical and socio-economic aspects

The dry stone walling, apparently simple in constructive terms, represents the work of many generations, whose origin is lost in time. According to Seva et al. (2005), the dry stone walls supporting small terraces appear, at least in eastern Spain, around the XVIII century B.C., with no direct relation to agriculture, and originally serving as shelter for shepherds in transhumance practices along the mountains. Moreover, for the Bronze Age,

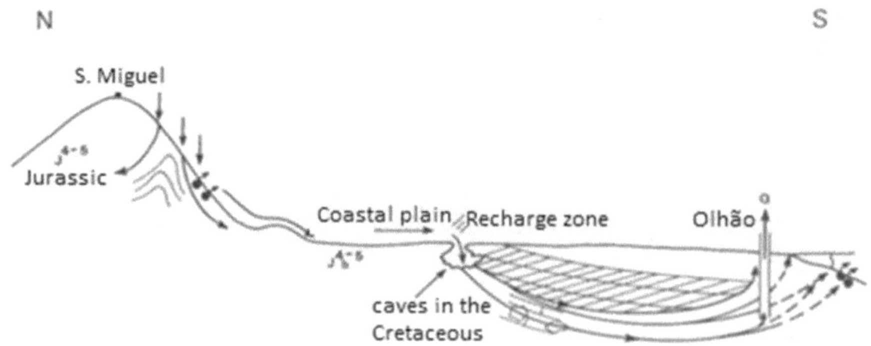

Source: Adapted from Costa et al. (1985)

Figure 4: Detail of hydraulic relations between limestone hills and littoral flat lands, northeast Faro

slope terracing is very well documented for Eastern Iberian Peninsula, mostly with the purpose of extending the household area (Asins-Velis 2006). However, the development of terracing for agricultural purposes appears in the Iberian Peninsula during the Roman times, with evidence from the first century B.C., and was further extend during the Muslim Andalusies presence, VIII-XIII centuries A.C. (Asins-Velis 2006).

In the case of the Algarve, the terraced dry orchards mainly includes fig, almond and carob trees, allowing leguminous crops under the tree crown cover, such as peas and beans, which help to incorporate nitrogen into the soil. Apart from providing food products to the populations, through the fruits and leguminous plants, carob and fig leaves are hay substitutes, which allow livestock (Feio 1983).

The development of such structures, common in many Mediterranean landscapes, for agricultural purposes mainly in the last three centuries, allowed population growth. In fact, the last period of terraced landscapes expansion occurs during 18th and 19th centuries (Guerny, Hsu 2010). At the Algarve region, however, at least in the mid-twentieth century, terraces were still in full expansion, primarily because the production of the installed fruit trees was much higher, in monetary terms, when compared to the cereal production. Around 1946-47, the production of figs, almonds, and carobs represented an important part of Portuguese exportations. The origins of such production is very ancient, already in the twelfth century A.C., the geographer and Arab botanist Edrisi, mentioned that the figs of Silves, the capital of the Algarve under the Moorish domination, were exported to all Western countries (Feio 1983).

Beyond the socioeconomic and historical interests, this kind of built agrosystem is extremely adaptive and generated new environmental equilibria, still relying on a continuous human intervention.

3.2 Building techniques

The construction techniques closely relates with permeability settings, allowing to redirect the water circulation and to enhance infiltration. Hence, the integrated building structure of terraces and dry stone walling define new waterways and influences land flows in a very soft manner.

Despite its apparent fragility, dry stone walling allows conditions of resistance and stability comparable to more technically modern structures like concrete walls, gabions, etc. Even from an economic point of view, dry stone retaining walls are competitive when walls are less than three meters high and even higher, when all environmental costs are accounted (Colas 2009). As for stability, this kind of walls can be included in a category of weight-walls, in which the support function is granted by the weight of the body wall that balances the landslide forces (Colas 2009, Villemus 2004).

No systematic work was found on the specific techniques used at the Algarve region,

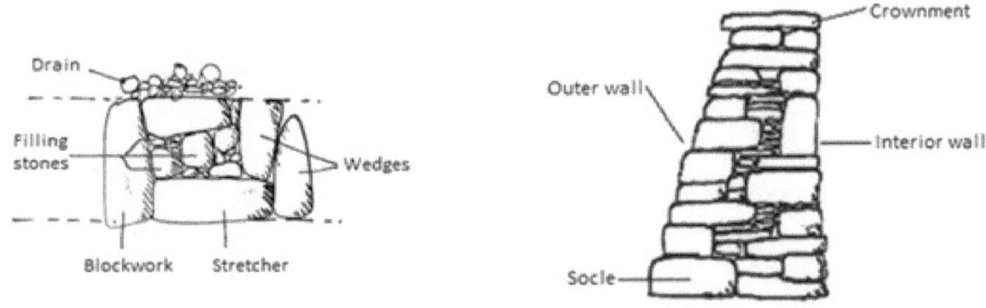

Source: Adapted from Colas (2009)

Figure 5: Building techniques. Left: Top view at the middle phase of a dry stone wall construction; Right: Cut view of a support wall

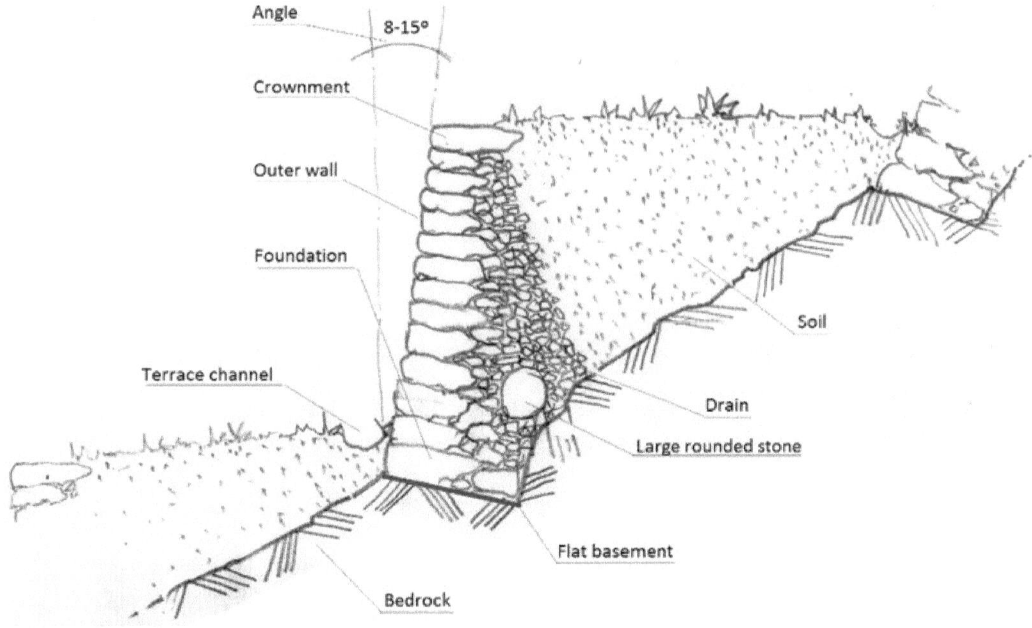

Source: Author's drawing, no scale, after Descazeaud et al. (2014) and Martini et al. (2004)

Figure 6: General scheme of a support dry stone wall

instead some field observations will be compared with documented studies for other Mediterranean regions. Although the great number of local variants, the basic technique is the placement of different types of stone in a way that they lock each other and fill interstitial spaces with thinner materials, thus improving drainage conditions (Figure 5, left).

A characteristic feature observable at the outer wall is the placement of hard materials on the basement, diminishing the size towards the top. As an indicative value but not a constructive rule, Martini et al. point to the following relation between width and height of the walls, in the case of Cinque Terre: 50 centimeters (cm) width of wall foundation for a maximum of 1,5 meters (m) height; about 70 cm width for 2-3m height and 80-100 cm for more than 3m. The outer wall has an inclination whose angle (fruit in French) will depend on its height, the type of soil and subsoil, rainfall and runoff (Figure 6). Colas (2009) references 8-15° for such angle, but other authors indicate 10-20° (Martini et al. 2004, Villemus 2004).

As stated by Larcena (2012), the walls work like a real sanitation network, letting the water pass over a kind of drain composed by smaller stones placed just behind the main body of the wall.

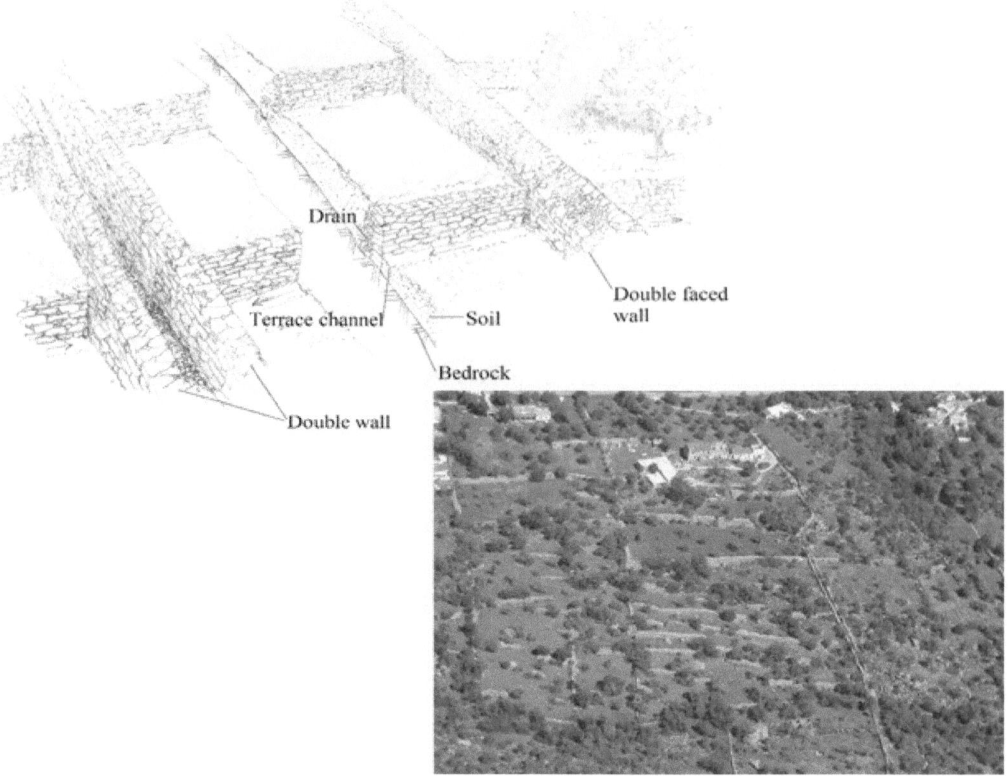

Source: Top left: Author's sketch, after Contessa (2014); no scale. Bottom right: Bragança (2006)

Figure 7: Drainage ditches. Top left: Drainage ditches in a terraced system. Bottom right: Photo near S. Brás de Alportel where double walling and other perpendicular walls are perfectly visible

The inherent fragilities due to the irregularity and the diminishing of resistance at the upper part of the wall lead to degradations over time and requires regular maintenance (Martini et al. 2004). However, drainage functions, particularly those assured at the lower part and even at the interior of the wall, guarantees the durability of most parts of the dry stone walling. For that reason, the wall basement prevents efficient drainage conditions, due to the concentration of large materials. Moreover, in some situations, the mixing of a few big rounded stones among smaller materials, just behind the basement, allows a better stability at the first row of the drainage process (Martini et al. 2004). In cases of more intensive rainfall, the definition of a terrace channel along the basement of the outer wall can happen, to help a better lateral runoff.

3.3 Hydraulic functions

A complex articulated set of walls shows a spatial modulation adapted to the preexisting relief modifies the natural water circulation, both in the vertical infiltration and the horizontal runoff. In fact, much of the water that infiltrates an upstairs terrace reaches the terrace downstairs, drained in the lateral sense, by a kind of micro channels carved under the walls (Larcena 2012). The definition of toe-channels is usual in areas of intense rainfall, but they are not evident on the barrocal of the Algarve region; however, some studies refer to a kind of channel with similar functions behind the crownment (Antão 2010).

Here, like in many other Mediterranean regions, the majority of walls present an alignment almost parallel to contour curves, but other wider walls cross them in a perpendicular or obliquus sense, allowing better stability and/or other functions. Such wider walls are double-faced walls, thus concentrating smaller materials inside.

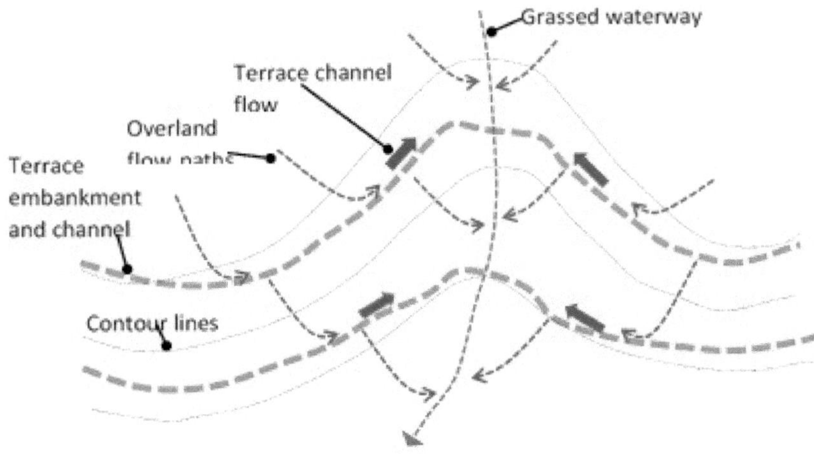

Source: Adapted from Foster (2004).

Figure 8: Scheme of the overland flows in a slope with terraced frame

Most of these walls mark the properties' boundaries, but they appear to receive and/or drain part of the lateral runoff. In some cases, such walls separate the lateral runoff. Figure 7 shows a general scheme for a case of a wider wall separating the lateral runoff. However, a double walling structure frequently helps the lateral runoff, thus mitigating the negative effects of soil erosion.

In an effective way, by receiving the water from terraces, the articulate set of drains have three functions: a) they break the torrential current in case of intense rainfall; b) they allow silt or sediment directing and c) they help to catch water that can be used for irrigation (Larcena 2012). It is true that at the barrocal infiltration is very important, but when torrential rainfall occurs, a part of the water runoff ends in little creeks or grassed waterways (Figure 8). Then, the sediment load (Foster 2004) intensifies, thus allowing the concentration of soils with better quality and moisture content along the small valleys, where there are some walls with less extensive design platforms, similar to the terrace slope embankments.

The walling is then far from a random spatial distribution. Rather, it shows a close relationship between biophysical characteristics and human intervention according to the needs of people (Reynès 2000). Figure 9 shows the adaptation of terraced structure to the topographic conditions on the barrocal. The soil deposition (Foster 2004) can be perceived along the small valley, although the shrubs do not allow a detailed view of drainage conditions. Despite the abandonment of a significant number of plots, the walling structure persists and subsistence activities are still present.

As mentioned above, the natural favorable conditions of water infiltration generates a complex set of aquifers. Less deep deposits allowed a great number of traditional wells and water springs that provided fresh water for human use and irrigation of small areas, because once it was not possible to exploit deep underground waters with traditional techniques.

We can also find some cases where clear interrelationships between walling structure and land use of valleys or other flat zones are evidently present. It is the case of small scale integrated systems of water springs, channels, water tanks for irrigation and mills, as shown in Figure 10.

3.4 Limitations and threats

In general terms, there is a great variety of constructive forms along all the walling structure, very well documented for most Mediterranean regions but not sufficiently systematized for the Algarve, including different techniques of stone preparing, crownment finishing, buttresses, access to platforms, combination with other rudimentary

Source: Image from Google maps 2017

Figure 9: Image of a small valley near Cerro de São Miguel, Northeast Faro

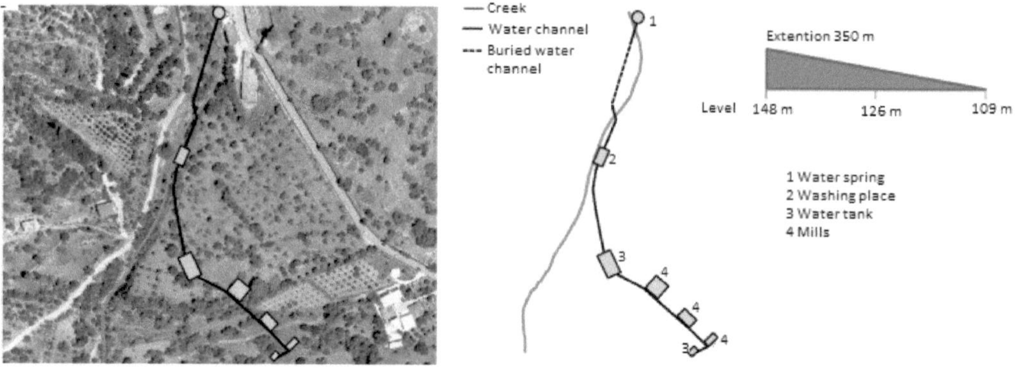

Source: Adapted from Barão (2014)

Figure 10: Hydraulic multifunctional system at Alface creek, north Faro

constructions, etc.

In addition to that, the landscape evaluation needs more specific studies about the hydraulic functioning, which are difficult to find, and about the ecological network associated to dry stone walling, including specific types of vegetation and cultural values. All such features relate closely with perceptive and symbolic aspects, it is easy to agree with Nohl's argument that "... aesthetic perception involves extracting information, knowledge and stories from the landscape, as much as possible. The more a beholder is successful at this, the greater is his emotional and expressive benefit." (Nohl 2001, p. 227).

As for the threats, they are very similar for all Mediterranean terraced landscapes. Following a scheme similar to that of Varotto (2008), one can identify three types of threats for the Algarve terraced landscapes: 1) lack of intervention; 2) excess of intervention and 3) creation of compensatory wilderness.

The first one relates to abandonment, the lack of stewardship by farmers[3] and the

---

[3]The Algarve follows the general trends registered at the national level: loss of more than 40% workers on agriculture in the decade form 2001-2011, as pointed out by the Instituto Nacional de Estatística. The situation gets worse at the case of terraces where the access is more difficult and the size of the plots hardly allows rentable farming.

disappearance of manual labor. Mechanized interventions are very difficult to develop when topographic characteristics are less advantageous. Then, the lack of intervention leads to the loss of large extensions of dry stone walling and terraces, affecting the set of complex interrelated functions. In the medium term, the domination of the garrigue[4], composed by bushes and poor quality woods, will cause a biodiversity reduction and will enhance the risks of fire hazards (Guerny, Hsu 2010). The disturbance of hydrogeological equilibrium by the lack of the dry walling structure conservation will affect the stability not only of slopes but also of some areas located downstream. As for cultural values, the loss of large dry stone walling extensions deprives the knowledge of traditional techniques and environmental adaptation of people developed over centuries.

The second type, the excess of intervention, has to do with the implementation of industrial agriculture, mostly orange orchards, and, above all, with the spread housing. The expansion of orange orchards occurred mainly from 1980 to 1990, supported by EU funds. As mentioned before, this land use occupies large areas precisely over the larger regional aquifer. Ironically, the regional land management plan, legally approved in 1991, classified the area as "imperative" zone for underground water protection (Bragança 2006). This kind of action illustrates "the diktat of the productivity and the banalization of the terraced landscapes" (Varotto 2008), once the more apt areas for agriculture production, at the littoral, were progressively absorbed by tourism and urban growth. The other excess derives from the housing spread that invades the front hills of the barrocal, whose arrangement form the amphitheater facing the coastal zone. The search for good or even idyllic views result in a jealous privatization[5] (Varotto 2008) of terraced landscape leading to the loss of identity and scenic attractiveness. Moreover, this contagious phenomenon has serious environmental and cultural impacts, not only by destroying or altering the dry stone walling, but also by affecting the quality and quantity of the underground water.

The 'urbanocentric' (Varotto 2008) perspective leads us to the third type of threats, the creation of compensatory wilderness. In fact, the metropolitan process of territorial organization induced by urban-tourism development, at the coastal zones, tends to spread artificialized spaces, which needs to be counterbalanced by establishing large areas for recreational use or encroachment of wilderness, normally with a positive meaning in ecological or romantic terms. As for the terraces, the concerns with protection for cultural reasons has been a common attitude between planners of some Mediterranean regions, without taking into account the complexity of its functions as a whole. It is not still the case for the Algarve, but there is a risk that the revision of the actual land management plans follow a similar practice of defining perimeters and establishing norms of conservation (Fontanari 2008).

4 Landscape's Reconstruction

The gap between the urban structures and the landscape is a key factor for future planning. It is an indubitable fact that, nowadays, the great majority of people live in metropolitan or pre-metropolitan[6] structures. This urban concentration tends to increase the distance between people and the surrounding places, which encompass a complex set of vital functions. As mentioned above, the involvement of people where they live is essential to design the sustainable conditions that can display new narratives and enhance poetic qualities of landscape (Nohl 2001).

---

[4]The garrigue comprehends scrublands developed from the progressive destruction of former persistent leaf forests on limestone hills. At the barrocal of Algarve, some of the most common shrubs and herbs are kermes oak (Quercus coccifera), rosemary (Rosmarinus officinalis), lavender (Lavanda sp.), honeysuckle (Lonicera implexa) pistachio (Pistacia lentiscus), some species of thymus and cistus.

[5]Terraces are private and, at the same time, community spaces. "The private property of the lands is strongly anchored to a collective system of maintenance and management that involves the structural, viability, hydraulic and productive aspects of the same." (Varotto 2008). Urbanites buy plots for building their individual resorts like being jealous of traditional adaptation.

[6]There is a tendency to consider groups of municipalities as metropolitan areas, although they do not present enough population nor urban structure. For the Algarve, a region with less than 500 000 resident inhabitants, the "GAMAL" –Great Metropolitan Area of Algarve– was officially created in 2004: the statutes have been published the 29 April on "Diário da República nº 101– III Série". In 2008, this denomination changed to "Comunidade Intermunicipal do Algarve" and the statues published the 19 December.

A central issue in this case will be the acknowledgment of specific features and values associated with the landscape terraces. "Not only did terraces have an ecological-environmental role –serving to develop certain techniques of construction, to protect terrain and to offer a locus for biodiversity– but they also had a clear socio-economic importance. These latter must be understood if we are to identify the reasons why such landscapes went into decline, and thence understand how they might once again become viable economic assets within the modern world." (Fontanari 2008, p. 10). Still, a crucial aspect of the landscape's reconstruction as a value is the recognition of its aesthetic importance for people, normally associated with subjectivity. However, despite the subjective nature of values, aesthetic preferences are not completely arbitrary. "New aesthetic orientations occur, as a rule, when significant landscape changes have taken place and when there is a population group who have strong, but no necessarily aesthetic interests in the new landscape." (Nohl 2001, p. 229).

4.1   An alternative process

At both a collective and an individual level, three main facets must be enhanced to understand the landscape and its evolution: perception, interpretation of the displayed scenery and the objective functioning of the visualized elements. Thus, the landscape construction is a process that involves both subjectivity, including social construction, and objectivity. Berque (1986) describes trajeçtion as the intimate involvement of the subject (human) and the object (physical/biological), like being two halves of the same reality. This means that the perception of environmental features by some societies is crucial in order to define the landscape. "Trajection means that things exist according to how we grasp them by the senses, by the thoughts, by the words and by the actions" (Berque 2013, p. 63).

Such understanding, apparently 'logical', challenges the typical dualism of the scientific paradigm: on the one side is the human subject who must observe and measure any object; on the opposite side is the concrete object to measure, where what cannot be measured does not physically exists. Contrariwise, according to Berque (2013), the human subject includes a prosthesis of technical and symbolic systems, which are part of its very constitution, in an 'eco-techno-symbolic' body. Then, everything will be both objective, the ecological and the technical, as well as subjective, the symbolic. Further, as stated by Watsuji, the relationship between a society and his environment is "the structural momentum of human existence" (Watsuji 2011). One must note that the momentum has the sense given by physics of mechanics, i.e. the power rating generated by a combination of two forces, in this case, the individual subject on one side, and his/her environment as his/her other half.

Somehow, this change of perspective undermines the common notion of 'natural landscape'. In fact, the 'natural' often arises as a reference for a visible and even imaginary nature that no longer exists, or that is succumbing to the constant aggression of a society that gradually broke up its ecological prosthesis. There is an illusion of fixing a standard unit, whereby one would measure the visible reality out of ourselves, hiding the effective conditions of degradation that is actually affecting all of us. However, as Bernard Kalaora points out, "contemporary nature cannot be conceived out of society, on the contrary it is grasped to all social phenomena" (Kalaora 1998, p. 17). Under this perspective, we will highlight an accordance of "global landscape" (Telles 1998) which embraces the interlinked urban and rural areas. These are the places where more people concentrate, with all the physical, biophysical, cultural, economic, and political environments that affects their own life.

Then, once the landscape is increasingly seen as a common good (Antrop 1999), the public participation in decision-making about the landscape evolution will be crucial. To this extent, a clear communication about the aspects involved in landscape transformation, leading to understand its complexity through soft models, will be essential, as will be referred to later.

4.2 Historical and philosophical background

For a better understanding of our perspective about landscape's evolution or reconstruction, we begin by a synthesis of some conceptual aspects, which regulate the meaning, the thought and the actions on landscape building in the professed Western world.

The Mediterranean environment, where Greek philosophy flourished, was the scenario of many metaphors and philosophical constructions. In the Greek world, the concept of city-region included all the space surrounding the human settlements. Such space supported and nourished the city itself, being part of the same unit that thrived as a whole. Thus, human communities depended on a space that fulfilled all their needs, not only food, lodging, but also aesthetic references, mental well-being, etc. Consequently, the space shaped by those communities, therefore being the matrix, like the mother, of the urban society, enclosed at the same time their print, like the son.

In a philosophical formulation of the world's organization, Plato in the Timaeus, proposed the term chôra to traduce metaphorically the reality of 'space - human community' relationships. He placed the term between the relative Being, genesis, which is born, lives and disappears and the absolute Being, idea, independent from time and space. Apart from the idea, the chôra feeds the genesis, which could not live without the chôra, both forming the sensible world, the kosmos. Thus, the chôra, i.e. the medium that surrounds the existent (Brisson 1998, Berque 2013), was both the one thing, the print, and its contrary, the matrix. Following Berque (2013), this was an aporia that Plato could not overcome, since he did not allow a third genus, triton allo genos, nor relative Being nor absolute Being, which he points out as the chôra.

The legacy of this aporia, which rejects the third genus, prevailed in the Aristotelian logic development and it is at the root of modern dualism with strong influences on Western thought. Indeed, this principle of 'the third excluded' still has a doubtful logical sense and influences the relationships between the human subject and his environment; individuals and society often consider their biophysical surrounds a perfect external entity. Then, according to Berque (2012), one ceases to relate the micro with the meso and the macro Kosmos, as intrinsic components of the human identity. Two classic references of modernism critics illustrate the dualistic approach: 1) in the view of Descartes thought, the environment would be considered a neutral object and 2) in Newtonian physics, an absolute object, homogeneous, isotropic and infinite (Naredo 1982). As a quick conclusion, the ontological foundations of modernism are referenced in the Timaeus.

The fact is that in modern societies, especially in metropolitan areas, where most people concentrate, the loss of a sense of Kosmos, derived from the ancient refusal of the third genus (triton allo genos), induces apprehensive 'allogeneic' conditions. Urban policies heavily exploit a landscape imagery that masks the propensity to ignore the human labor, which generated the real landscapes and direct attention to beautiful and ideal 'natures' (Donadieu 2012). From the perspective of Berque's mesological geography, the liberal capitalist economy takes advantage of the popular trend to copy the position of elites wagered on making the work invisible for society (Donadieu 2012).

Hence, we witness an individualism-based system, in which the human subject cuts the links to the medium that surrounds him, thus separating a physical/eco body from his eco-techno-symbolic entirety (Berque 1986). The loss of a human sense of the places where people dwell is a consequence of breaking such existential ties that bind people to an autonomous interpretation of the real landscape. In contrast, urban societies ends up conditioned by fétiche objects and spaces. This explains why people do not react to cities with unscaled architectures, social environments of increasing inequality, segregated and guarded urban life, unreliable food supplies, fictitious land management plans and environmental conditions constantly deteriorating (Donadieu 2012).

4.3 Towards 'kosmic' or utopic landscapes

It is difficult to ignore this globalized and virtualized world with no apparent way out, lacking real pathways towards more sustainable solutions. We are then compelled to agree on a philosophical 'back to basics' regarding the recuperation of a common sense of 'kosmos', now applied to actual urban structures. Such sense of 'kosmos' is the sense of landscape. From this perspective, we place two main questions regarding the landscape evolution: 1) how can we take a step forward? and 2) how can we discover alternative ways?

In a common sense, dreams command life and, like in many other similar situations in the history humankind, utopias can be very useful. As Donadieu (2012) notes, utopias suggest virtual and rational worlds, they are not predictions nor forecasts, they just build a virtual society without having a geographical location. This author distinguishes two types of operational utopias, which try to move from dream to reality, both pursuing the common values for wellbeing, living and thinking: the chimerical and the realistic ones. The first type of utopias rely on dogmatic beliefs, specific to dualistic views and, when achievable, usually have a high price. History, not so distant, of National Socialism or regimes inspired by dogmatic Marxism provides significant examples. The second type, the realistic utopias, with no aporias nor social dramas, pursue the access to common wealth based on solidarity and mutual respect.

As stated by Petrella, "The object of the common good is the common wealth, i.e. the set of principles, rules, institutions and resources that promote and guarantee the existence of all the members of a human community. On the intangible level, one of the elements of the common good comprises the triptych recognition-respect-tolerance in relations with the other. In material terms, the common good is structured around the right to fair access for all to food, housing, energy, education, health, transport, information, democracy and artistic expression." (Petrella 1996, p. 13). According to this author, the Welfare State, already experienced after the great crisis of 1929, designates the aspiration to the common good based on solidarity, thus being an example of a realistic utopia.

One may also look to sustainability and urban sustainability as realistic utopias, being the endpoint that we seek, but never reach (Forman 2008). However, the scale is actually one of the key issues to make a realistic utopia operational, in a way that people can have an effective participation with common goods management. The huge gap between the citizens and the decision-making centers, as well as the prevailing strategies based on the maximization of the investor's profits, back to capitalism 1.0[7], are strong barriers, and block new evolutions.

The search for a proper spatial and temporal scale where we are able to cause specific changes in order to move towards a better world will then face us with what Forman (1995) calls the management paradox: "Small spaces are easily changed, but inherently unstable. Large spaces are hard to change, yet have considerable stability." (Forman 2008, p. 316). When focusing on mid-size spaces, such as landscapes and regions, one's improvement efforts achieves an effect that can be visible on the short term and can persist in the long term. Like trying to take care of our own garden, we should think, "Landscapes and regions are simply big gardens to be invested in and cared for." (Forman 2008, p. 316).

In that sense, Forman (2008) proposes the concept of urban-region, looking where best to focus efforts for an effective mesh of nature and people in and around cities. The intention is to apply the concept to the places in which more than 50% of world population currently concentrates. In the urban-region scheme, the part with less ecological functions corresponds to the hole of a donut, an empty space having several forms, and the part with highest bio-ecological potential and landscape value, corresponds to the ring forming the sugary mass of the same donut (Figure 11).

Based on an exploration of 38 examples of urban regions around the world, Forman (2008) reasserts some of the fundamentals already proposed by other planners of the early twentieth century, like Patrick Geddes, Fredrick Olmsted or Lewis Mumford. Such principles emerged from the need of restoring the interdependence between the urban

---

[7]Capitalism 1.0 is a first phase of capitalism system also known as free-market or 'laissez-faire', in which the politic power had a poor intervention; the interactions between governments and private companies were guided by the guarantee of military revenue and consequent protection of powerful interests. Some well-known facets of this period are the phenomenal economic growth, but also the cruel exploitation of workers and the environmental degradation. "... in the early capitalist era, land, resources, and places to dump wastes were abundant; aggregated capital was the scarcest factor. That's why rules and practices developed that put capital above all else." (Barnes 2006, p. 24)

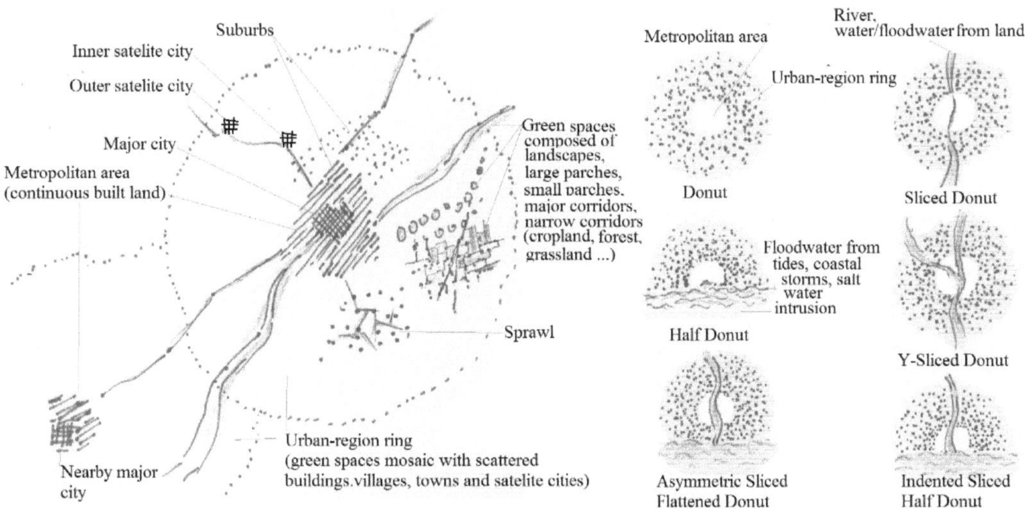

Source: Sketch by the author after Forman (2008).

Figure 11: Left: Concepts and terms for urban-regions; Right: Donut model

structure and the surrounding area that can support and feed the human settlements.

One can relate these concerns to the philosophical problem raised by Plato in the Timaeus, concerning the chôra. However, the unsustainable, even irreversible, state of big metropoles makes them the actual aporias, with no way out. Donadieu (2012), for example, states the unsustainable future of cities without close vicinity agriculture, thus inverting the aporias sense refused by Plato. This means that the future will depend on a third genus able to unify the matrix and the footprint of the existent human communities. In this sense, Donadieu conceives the 'Agropolia', an alternative urban world with agriculture and farmers, as a utopia similar to the urban-region proposed by Forman (2008).

4.4   The Utopic landscape of the Algarve

To this extent, the implementation of the urban world's existential vision in 'Agropolia' must explicitly reach two fundamental aspects. On the one hand, the perception of landscapes and places must be free from imposed cultural patterns, allowing their display as they are, understood and admired to get a satisfaction beyond the amorphous comfort and aesthetic pleasure of spectacles. On the other hand, the development of the sensitivity is crucial to resume the ties that bind people to the environment in which they live and to overcome the fetish choices inculcated by experts that stimulate consumption.

In physical terms, the description of this imaginary region is as follows, "Agropolia is not an island, but an archipelago of Urban Spaces built among the fields, parks, forests and ponds. There is a free access by railways and highways, through ports and airports. Beyond Agropolia, the ocean extends on one side and, on the opposite side there is a barrier of wooded mountains intersected by rural valleys sparsely populated." (Donadieu 2012, p. 285).

Such a description fits to the urban-touristic zone of Algarve (Figure 12), which is formally a polynuclear urban zone where we can identify the following basic components:

1. the donut hole of its urban region correspond to the continuous built mass formed by traditional urban centers and by urban settlements for tourism purposes;

2. the ring of the donut is the miscellaneous formed by urban sprawl, villages and little towns, green spaces (golf courses, wooded and agriculture areas, wetlands, etc.); and

3. the limit to the south is the Atlantic ocean and the northern boundary is formed by the shale mountains.

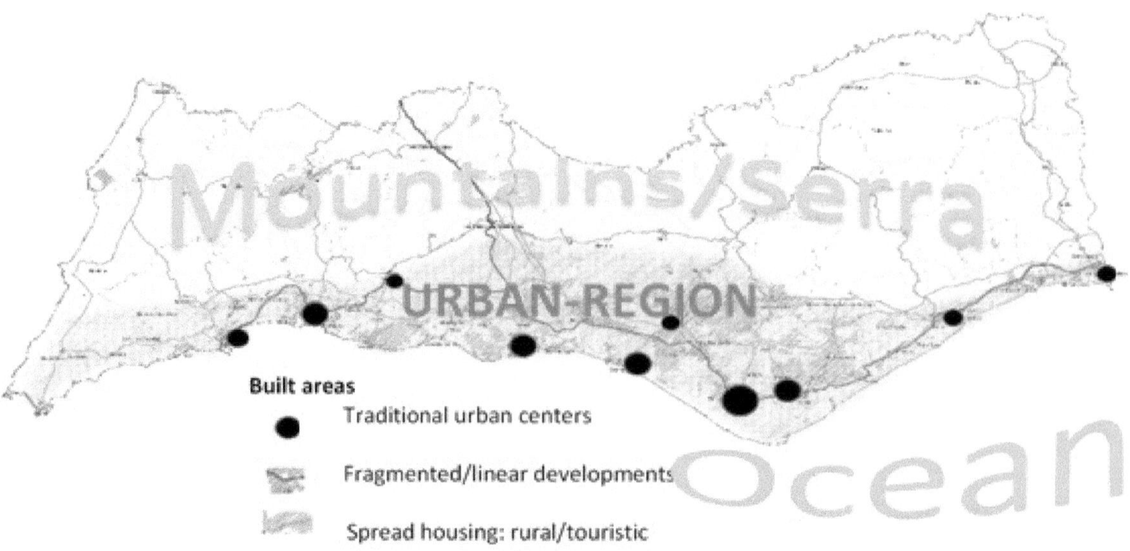

Source: Sketch by the author, no scale, using "peça gráfica 08, anexos volume 1" of the regional land management plan of Algarve (CCDRAlgarve. 2007)

Figure 12: The urban-region of Algarve. Main components and barriers; spectral zone

Undeniably, the coastal zone of the Algarve, as well as its background area has plenty of problems such as urban densification, bad locations, stressed sensible areas, aesthetic disharmony, etc. Nevertheless, the focus on this utopic urban-region may allow us an adequate scale for improving the actual situation, thus overcoming the management paradox and considering the landscape as the second half of the communities that live there. This perspective is quite different from that of landscape units. Our approach intends to look at landscape far from a closed entity that eventually achieves an optimal state to which one could compare and measure the impacts of human actions. Rather, we intent to reach an agreement about landscapes as special regions, once "...landscape descriptions are always biased. Furthermore, it is not possible to accurately define this bias, because there is no neutral ground from which a bias (or its extent) can objectively identified. In a relational view, however, (potential) biases can at least be put in a relation with each other and can be negotiated. As a consequence, landscape planning and development must be based on and geared towards negotiations of different trajectories and between different notions and stakeholders." (Backhaus 2011, p. 195).

5   Rehabilitation and Renewal of Terraced Landscape

It is under this perspective that we intend to prospect the future of dry walling as a structural element of landscape. Although we cannot witness a visual exuberance of the Algarve hills, the terrace frame, supported by the dry stone walling, can embody an aesthetical positive view for many perceptions. Furthermore, terraces are the base of an agrosystem with great ecological and cultural values. Hence, we try to reach the symbolic, aesthetic, cultural and ecologic values that the society needs to adopt.

The encouragement of public participation in a very effective way is crucial to prospect the ways for rehabilitation or renovation actions. Then, we need to support in a method that facilitates communication, to stimulate the citizen's participation in landscape evolution. In fact, there is a need to communicate perceptions and conceptions of landscapes as clearly as possible, in order to raise awareness and initiate processes of participation, and thus serve as a contribution to ethical discourse on landscape development (Hansen 2001).

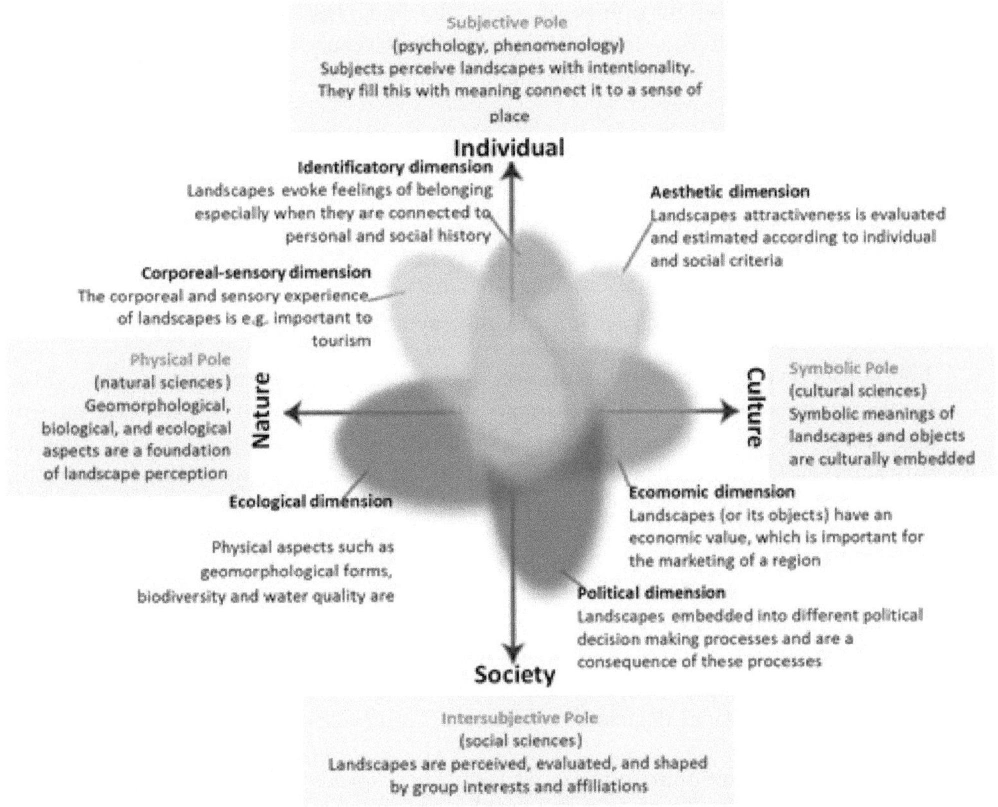

Source: Adapted from Backhaus (2011)

Figure 13: The four pole model with its six dimensions of landscape experience

5.1 *Explanatory model of landscape*

In that sense, we try to get closer to the guidelines of the explanatory model developed within the Swiss National Research Program 48 "Landscapes and Habitats of the Alps" (Backhaus et al. 2008), which includes a multidimensional approach, in which insights are shared and connected across the boundaries of disciplines. An important feature is to allow the location of different approaches of landscape perception.

The model's structure follows two main axes connecting four poles[8]. Once landscape perception and experience occurs between nature and culture, the first axe goes from nature to culture, because the role of landscape in mediating between the natural environment and human activity depends on acquired rules, models, and cultural patterns. The second axe goes from individual to society, because each individual has their own perception of the landscape as a part of a society that organizes and manages the space appropriated by different social groups. "The field that stretches between these four poles encompasses different kinds of approaches to and perceptions of landscapes. While every access to landscapes includes aspects of every pole, certain approaches tend to be drawn towards one or another pole." (Backhaus 2011, p. 196). Figure 13 sketches the two polarities and the six dimensions.

We then have four poles: physical, subjective, symbolic and intersubjective, which are described in detail below.

A) The physical pole refers to what people generally first perceive when beholding a landscape: arable land, rivers, woodlands, settlements, roads, animals, machines; however, landscape perception do not happen per se, in an 'objective' way, rather

---

[8]More than the three layers of landscape stated by Berque (1986), the biophysical, the subjective and the social, the model introduces a fourth layer or pole, considering cultural and intersubjective as separate poles. The main reason is to offer "...the possibility of better showing where the socio-cultural tensions, rifts, and disruptions are that determine landscapes today." (Backhaus et al. 2008, p. 134)

resulting from different points of view. In fact, the natural flows and complex relations between living elements reveals the existence of many invisible or hidden aspects; the release or acknowledgement of such aspects may change the experience of beholders (Backhaus 2011).

B) The symbolic pole, at the opposite side of the axis, relates then with the cultural patterns, aesthetics and symbols that mediate people's perception and experience of the world and landscapes. Alterations of landscapes that oppose shared, often traditional, aesthetic notions are not easily accepted (Backhaus 2011). The art and media, for example, have an important role in transmitting patterns that are not merely instruments of perception but also systems of interpretation.

C) The subjective pole comprehends, on the one hand, the subject as the center of emotions, sensations and perceptions. Subjects intentionally grasp their surroundings using not only the visual sense but also all the other senses. On the other hand, this same pole also comprehends the subjects referred to as individuals within a society, individuals choosing the aspects of landscape that arouse their interest.

D) The intersubjective pole, at the opposite side of the axis, takes then into account the landscape as a product of social practices such as agriculture, trade, leisure, etc. Explicitly, landscape clearly involves economic factors such as the landscape as a resource with use value or market value, a sense of belonging and authenticity, a social history of representation, insiders and outsider's perspective, and political aspects like a political decision's impacts on landscape development.

We will explore some connections between these poles for the case of the Algarve urban region, as a way to detect some possible perceptions that can be useful for future discussions among stakeholders. In this sense, we expose some sketches used by Donadieu (2008) for terraced landscapes. Nevertheless, it will be necessary to pursue a more detailed fieldwork to explore the dimensions pointed by the four poles method and reach "...an ethical discourse that includes a mandate for the protection and shaping of landscapes" (Backhaus et al. 2008).

5.2 Main trends and possible evolutionary prospects

Following the Donadieu (2008) scheme, we point out two trends more or less pursued: the abandonment and the conservation of functionality. The abandonment, which occurs in most cases, has to do, on the one hand with the rural exodus to the cities and tourist centers and, on the other hand, the difficulties of modernization and agricultural techniques due to steep slopes, cost of hand labor, marketing alternatives. The conservation of functionality, increasingly less frequent, may be related with the Common Agricultural Policy (CAP) aids to subsistence agriculture, but also with maintained activity by traditional farmers, or even modern farmers in the case of some farms being economically sustainable.

At this point, we must search for three alternatives. Firstly, we may think about assigning a patrimonial value to terrace landscapes, under a statute of cultural landscapes. In such a situation, these landscapes are likely to fall into oblivion, 'collective amnesia', or stay as a souvenir object, 'anamnesis'. It might even happen through classification as world heritage sites, or inclusion in museum figurines of planet cultures.

Therefore, as a second possibility, it might be necessary to place landscapes into value through the image, i.e. by aestheticizing them, even if such landscapes do not exhibit any special attributes. This would occur within tourism interests, by artializing the landscape (Roger 1997) via image and text descriptions, then creating beauty, excitement and spectacle. With fewer chances, we would consider an enhancement through agricultural economy, shaping the landscape in order to make it more attractive, not only for the 'excellency' of the products obtained, but also for the aesthetics.

As a third possibility, one can consider to recover abandoned terraces or even to create new platforms. For the barrocal of the Algarve, we could think about unique branded goods such as 'unique Algarve orange', famous Silves fig, etc., like the Oporto vineyards in the north of Portugal or the Cassis vineyards in France. In a touristic environment like

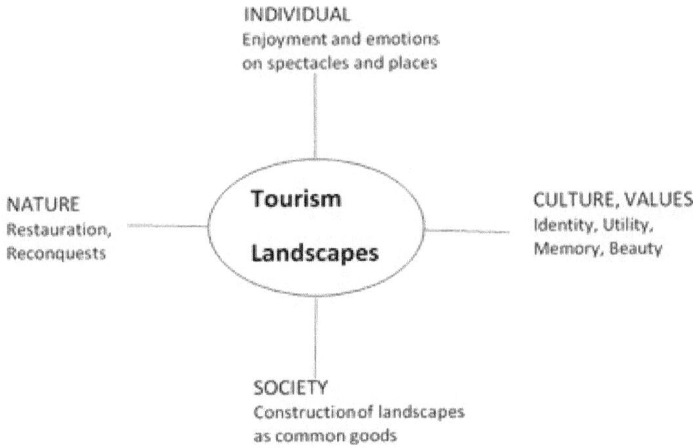

Source: Adapted from: Backhaus et al. (2008) and Donadieu (2008)

Figure 14: The four pole model for tourism landscapes

the Algarve, the promotion of cultural and tourist circuits could be more plausible; once a change from linear developments to non-linear ones is not expected, a combination of several solutions would be necessary.

In short, we can have the following typologies: 1) landscapes of abandonment and 'oblivion'; 2) patrimonial landscapes or 'collective memory'; 3) cultural landscapes promoted by recognition/artialization of unique places, notable, or even common places 4) highly valued landscapes of individual economic profitability; 5) landscapes of 'reconquest', including the addition of types 2 + 3 + 4.

5.3   Tourism landscapes

Once tourism is the driving force of the Algarve land planning, the attraction for the future fate of this region will be to embrace the dynamics of tourism landscapes. Then, the main goal of the intersubjective strategy for the urban region, in which the barrocal is the 'living' part (ecologically speaking), lead by the interest groups linked to tourism, will be the construction of landscapes as common goods (Figure 14). Taking the other sense of the axis, the framework of individual perceptions of enjoyment and emotions on spectacles and places will conform the societal strategy of building the landscape as a common good, prejudging the individual demands of enjoyment and excitement. Therefore, rehabilitation and 'reconquest' should respect the cultural features and identity values that invoke collective memory and convey beauty.

When looking for practical possibilities of recovery, restoration or 'reconquest', a key question one should put, drawing inspiration from Neuray (1992), is to know exactly who the recipients of these landscapes are. It will be then imperative to take into account the various ways of looking at the landscape, within different sensitivities, learning and training. In that sense, Donadieu (2008) considers landscapes as:

1. The perceptions / 'looks' trained in relation to the beauty and landscape art, aestheticians, outsiders, exogenous, including here most of the tourists;

2. The initiated looks in relation to the rules of local life, which will be insiders, endogenous, including here much of the urban population;

3. The perceptions / 'looks' informed by material and immaterial production of landscapes, corresponding to scientific looks.

This does not mean that every way of looking corresponds to a specific type of local landscape, although some landscapes will appeal more to certain ways of looking than others. For example, the trained 'looks', usually attributed to tourists, tend to value

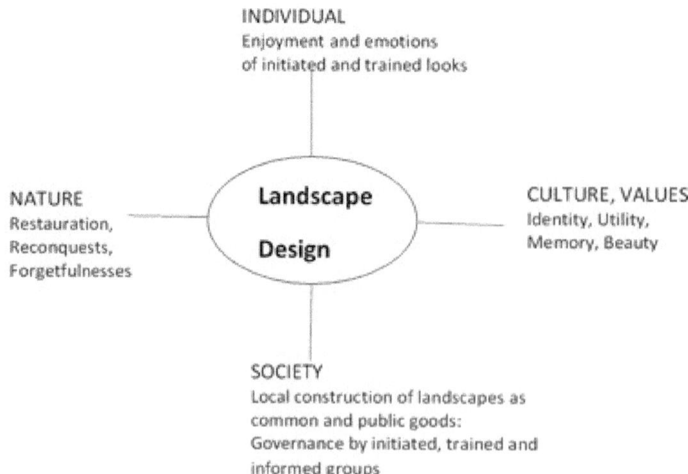

Source: Adapted from: Backhaus et al. (2008) and Donadieu (2008)

Figure 15: The four pole model for landscape design

scenarios with more formal splendor and contrasts –Machu Pichu in Peru, the rice field terraces in Asia, the Portuguese Douro valley vineyards, etc. However, a landscape with an impressive visual effect over a traditional compact city will have similar valuations by many trained looks from tourists, initiated looks from urbanites and farmers, and informed looks from agronomists, biologists, architects, landscape architects, etc.

Therefore, the local construction of landscape, sketched and promoted on a regional scale, will require a shared governance between initiated, trained and informed social groups. Taking the spectrum of the vertical axis (Figure 15), the individual perceptions based on the enjoyment and emotions of initiated and trained looks will integrate the intersubjective construction of local landscapes as common and public goods. The satisfaction of the various looks that will contemplate such planned landscapes must necessarily take into account the cultural values –identity, utility, beauty and memory. This will influence the several typologies of resulting local landscapes, according to the natural conditions under such cultural features; one must concretely think about designing local landscapes that can be rehabilitated or regained and, at the same time, imbalance those that will be forgotten, such as patrimony and 'collective amnesia'.

5.4 Landscape's governance

Then the following crucial question is about the real terms of governance to implement. According to Donadieu (2008), in the current situation, one can consider three essential facets:

1. The legislative injunction, top-down arising from the European Landscape Convention and the respective transpositions into national legislation;

2. The self-sustainable local initiatives (Magnaghi 2000), bottom-up;

3. The local governance landscape projects, bottom-up and top-down.

As for the legislative injunction, one can recall, for example, some articles of the European Landscape Convention:

- artº 1 a) [Landscape] "... an area, as perceived by people, ...";

- artº 1 b) ""Landscape quality objective" means, for a specific landscape, the formulation by the competent authorities of the aspirations of the public ...";

- artº 6 c) "Identification and assessment" 1 "With the active participation of the interested parties ...".

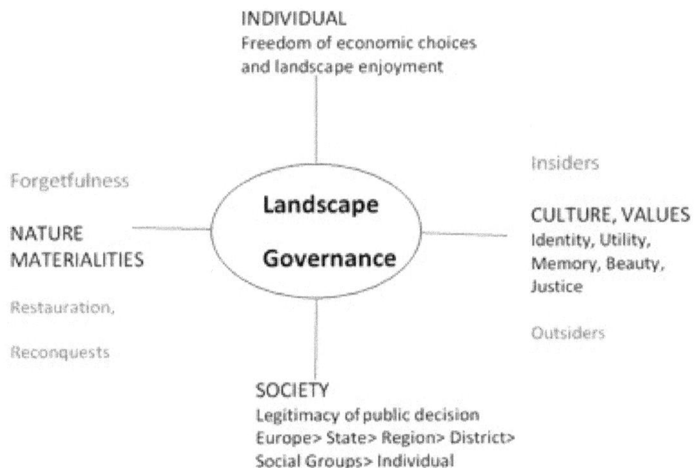

Source: Adapted from: Backhaus et al. (2008) and Donadieu (2008)

Figure 16: The four pole model for landscape governance

The influence of public authorities on modeling the perception and the formulation of the aspiration of the public can easily happen, despite the call for the active participation of interested parties. In fact, for the Algarve region, we have detected many problems in terms of active public participation (Bragança 2006). Here the top-down practices prevailed in the conventional land planning and management processes, once decision-making fulfils a legitimacy ritual based on descending disclosure of information, consultation and conciliation attempt.

As a typical example of top-down governance for terraced landscapes, Donadieu (2008) mentions George Brassens Public Park in Paris, recreating terraced vineyards of XIX century, with non-commercial purposes. Similarly, it is easy to imagine a decision –from the central or local authorities– about the reuse of some terraced dry orchard of Algarve's barrocal as merely recreational areas aesthetically designed for satisfying coastal urbanites and mass tourism.

Bottom-up governance implies a delegation of decisions to local communities, which have the autonomy and the chance to pursue a participatory local democracy. Hobby farming can provide some examples in this case. For the Algarve urban region one could imagine some associative initiatives of urban citizens that live in coastal cities, forming communities whose aim would be to enjoy farming on barrocal, thus reactivating traditional practices similar to permaculture. They would buy or rent some properties and explore the dry orchard products mainly for personal needs, including the conservation of their cultural identity.

Merging top-down and bottom-up implies to interchange information, co-decision making and involvement in management. It can be the case of some projects promoted by local or regional institutions satisfying the ambitions of local representative agents or communities, who actively collaborate in the promotion and continuity of such projects. One might imagine a project for promoting the 'Algarvian' almond or carob as products of excellence, unique, designed by the regional university and prioritized by the regional authorities, as the result of the lobbying exercised by a significant group of farmers and other social agents who are conscious of real dry orchards value. Such a project could easily take advantage of the possibilities provided by EU funds.

The options about the arrangement for landscape governance will derive from individual freedom of economic choices, framed by the legitimacy of public decisions (Figure 16). The cultural values of identity, utility, collective memory, beauty and justice guide the options for the management of physical, biophysical, material reality. Such values closely relate to the ethical patterns[9] of insiders and outsiders that can reinforce the restoration,

---

[9] As noted by Hansen (2001, p. 247): "Ethical norms are usually associated with what values are to be realised." Moreover, "To value something is to make moral decisions, and moral decisions build on ethical

'reconquest' and/or forgetfulness of local landscapes.

The restauration and renewal of dry stone walling structure will depend on numerous options sketched using the landscape as an instrument of knowledge and acknowledgement of the regional space. Even considering tourism landscape, our focus on the urban-touristic region of Algarve enhances the landscape as a common good. To that extent, one must overcome the nostalgic statement and try to redevelop landscape as a viable locus of a modern way of life (Fontanari 2008). Then, the looks of insiders and outsiders will condition the aesthetic features of regional landscape design, taking into account that "the principles derived from the recognized aesthetic values embodied by terraced landscape should be applied in the construction of new landscapes of which terraces are a crucial central component." (Fontanari 2008, p. 12), once "local communities have certain "rights" over such local assets." (Fontanari, Patassini 2008, p. 7). The three main types of local units that may emerge from designing the regional landscape are: 1) restoration; 2) 'reconquest' and 3) forgetfulness. They all entail governance systems derived from the negotiations between different notions and stakeholders; however, the bottom-up and mixed bottom-up and top-down styles seems to be more adapted to manage the future landscape.

6   Final Remarks

We actually follow a process of evolution in landscape policies that requires changes at social, cultural and individual levels (Backhaus et al. 2008). It is not easy to overcome the dualistic matrix that conditions the Western way of thinking and acting. In a progressive way, however, the current changes leads to incorporating more intangible aspects on landscape design and development. By rejecting the actual aporias of unsustainable cities and metropolitan areas, design processes necessarily face us with realistic utopias, both at local/regional levels and globally. As suggested by Forman (2008), we even can take 'big pictures', global sustainable scenarios, into account: "Think Globally, Plan Regionally, and Then Act Locally. Keep the globe in mind when making daily decisions. But most importantly, create a plan for every landscape and every region that provides sustainably for nature and people. Then with the broad plan in hand, make the important local changes and refinements that fit effectively into the big picture." (Forman 2008, p. 317).

In the case of the Algarve urban region, which hallmark was its terraced landscape supported by a dry stone walling structure, the first step will be an effective knowledge of its physical presence and significance. For the physical aspects, we mean extension, adaptation to topography, forms and aesthetic combinations; for the significance, we mean symbolic, technological, ecological, economic values. Such aspects received a poor attention from the public institutions responsible for land planning and management, despite the cascade of plans that emerged in the last three decades. A second step will be to pave the way for more democratic forms of governance, bottom-up or merged top-down and bottom-up, encouraging collective actions or concerted design projects, thus overcoming the typical top-down mechanisms of conventional plans.

Unless the dry stone walling structure of the Algarve becomes part of a patrimonial set of the Mediterranean typical coastal landscapes, the lack of its spectacular appearance surely make difficult its recognition as a world heritage. This does not detract the importance of strengthing its cultural value by the people that coexist in this landscapes. In view of actual interest groups, it appears plausible that tourism can provide a valuable support towards an 'artialization' (Roger 1997), thus enhancing all symbolic values and making patrimonial value easier to be recognized. In that sense, many looks must be initiated, particularly among urbanites. It will then be possible to rehabilitate and renew a large part of dry stone walling of the Algarve urban-tourist region, despite the difficulty from learning how to forget and to reassign new values to the landscape that may display new narratives and enhance its poetry (Nohl 2001).

---

considerations. ... By involving the public in general together with different types of experts and those who live in the landscapes in question, or who use them in different ways, these different groups will have opportunities to influence the ethical discourse by reasonable arguments." (Hansen 2001, p. 252).

References

Antão T (2010) O espaço de habitar vernacular no barrocal algarvio. Master's thesis. departamento de arquitetura. escola de artes. universidade de Évora.

Antrop M (1999) Background concepts for integrated landscape analysis. *Agriculture, Ecosystems and Environment* 77: 17–28. CrossRef.

Asins-Velis S (2006) Linking historical mediterranean terraces with water catchment, harvesting and distribution structures. In: Morel JP, Jordi J, Matamala J (eds), *The archaeology of crop fields and gardens*. Edipuglia s.r.l., Barcelona, 21–40

Backhaus N (2011) Landscapes, spatial totalities or special regions? *Procedia Social and Behavior Sciences* 14: 193–202. CrossRef.

Backhaus N, Reichler C, Stremlow M (2008) Conceptualizing landscape: An evidence-based model with political implications. *Mountain Research and Development* 28[2]: 132–139. CrossRef.

Barnes P (2006) *Capitalism 3.0 - Guide to reclaiming the commons*. Berrett-Koehler Publishers, Inc., San Francisco

Barão M (2014) Linhas de água (re)construídas no barrocal algarvio. Sistemas de reaproveitamento de água de nascente para rega e moagem. master's thesis. departamento de artes e humanidades. faculdade de ciências humanas e sociais. universidade do algarve.

Berque A (1986) *Le sauvage et l'artifice - Les Japonais devant la nature*. Gallimard, Paris

Berque A (2012) La chôra chez platon. Em t. p. (dir.), espace et lieu dans la pensée occidentale de platon à nietzche (pp. 13-27). la découverte. paris. what is this?

Berque A (2013) Tétralemme et milieu humain : la mésologie à la lumière de yamauchi. *Ebisu* 49: 57–71. CrossRef.

Bragança C (2006) Metodología para la evaluación de sistemas territoriales. aplicación al sistema hidrológico-hidráulico del algarve. Ph.d. thesis. departamento de geografía humana. facultad de geografía e história. universidad de sevilla

Braudel F (2001) *Memórias do Mediterrâneo. Pré-história e Antiguidade*. Terramar, Lisbon

Brisson L (1998) *Le même et l'autre dans la structure ontologique du Timée de Platon*. Academia Verlag, Sankt Augustin

CCDRAlgarve. (2007) Plano regional de ordenamento do território do algarve. Acceded in 24 of february 2017 on the web site of comissão de coordenação e desenvolvimento regional do algarve: http://www.prot.ccdr-alg.pt/download.aspx

Colas AS (2009) Mécanique des murs de soutènement en pierre sèche: modélisation par le calcul à la rupture et expérimentation échelle 1. Ph.d. thesis. École centrale de lyon. université de lyon

Contessa V (2014) Terraced landscapes in italy: state of the art and future challenges. Master's thesis. dipartamento territorio e sistemi agro-forestali. università degli studi di padova

Costa E, Brites J, Pedrosa M, Silva A (1985) *Carta hidrogeologica da orla algarvia*. Serviços Geológicos de Portugal, Lisbon

Descazeaud M, Faraggi T, Soulage J (2014) Murs de soutenement - comparaison environnementale et financière de différentes technologies. École centrale lyon

Donadieu P (2008) Terraced landscapes in europe: Why, for whom and how? Alpter final conference. ljubljana. acceded in 24 of june 2015 on the web site of alpter project: http://www.alpter.net/img/pdf/2˙donadieu˙ljubljana˙07.pdf

Donadieu P (2012) As paisagens agriurbanas: uma utopia realista? In: Veríssimo Serrão A (ed), *Filosofia e Arquitetura da paisagem. Um manual.* Centro de Filosofia da Universidade de Lisboa, Lisbon

Feio M (1983) *Le Bas Alentejo et l'Algarve.* Centro de Ecologia Aplicada da Universidade de Évora, Évora

Fontanari E (2008) A move beyond nostalgia. In: Fontanari E, Patassini D (eds), *Terraced Landscapes of the Alps. Projects in progress.* Marsilio Editori, Venice, 10–13

Fontanari E, Patassini D (2008) Introduction. In: Fontanari E, Patassini D (eds), *Terraced Landscapes of the Alps. Projects in progress.* Marsilio Editori, Venice, 7

Forman R (1995) *Land Mosaics: The Ecology of Landscapes and Regions.* Cambridge University Press, New York

Forman R (2008) *Urban Regions. Ecology and Planning Beyond the City.* Cambridge University Press, New York

Foster BG (2004) Terraces and terracing. *Encyclopedia of soils in the environment* 4: 135–143

Guerny J, Hsu L (2010) Terraced landscapes: Meeting to challenges to sustainability. A nothern mediterranean agriculture perspective. first terraced landscape conference. honghe, china

Hansen B (2001) Ethics and landscape: Values and choices. *Ethics, Place and Environment* 4[3]: 246–252

Kalaora B (1998) *Au-delà de la nature, l'environnement. L'observation sociale de l'environnement.* L'Harmattan, Paris

Larcena D (2012) Terrasses et eau des versants en méditerranée; dynamiques Écologiques et Économiques. In: Aspe C (ed), *De L'eau Agricole À L'eau Environnementale. Résistence et Adaptation Aux Noveaux Enjeux de Partage de L'eau En Méditerranée.* Éditions Quae, Versailles, 241–252

Lasanta T, Arnáez J, Flaño P, Monreal N (2013) Los bancales en las montañas españolas: un paysaje abandonado y un recurso potencial. *Boletín de la asociación de geógrafos españoles* 63: 301–322

Machado J (1991) *Grande Dicionário da Língua Portuguesa.* Publicações Alfa

Magnaghi A (2000) *Il progetto locale.* Bollati Boringhieri, Torino

Martini S, Pesce G, De Franchi R, Colombo R, Tavaroli F (2004) Manuale per la construzioni dei muri a secco. linee guida per la manutenzione dei terrazzamenti delle cinque terre. http://www.alpter.net/img/pdf/manuale˙recupero.pdf

Naredo J (1982) La ordenación del territorio: sus presupuestos y perspectivas en la actual crisis de civilización. Cursos de ordenación del territorio. madrid

Neuray G (1992) *Des paysages. Pour qui?. Pourquoi?. Comment?* Les presses agronomiques de Gembloux, Gembloux

Nohl W (2001) Sustainable landscape use and aesthetic perception-preliminary reflections on future landscape aesthetics. *Landscape and Urban Planning* 54: 223–237. CrossRef.

Oteros J (2014) Modelización del ciclo fenológico reproductor del olivo. Ph.d. thesis. servicio de publicaciones de la universidad de córdoba

Petrella R (1996) *Le Bien commun. Éloge de la solidarité*

Reynès A (2000) Patrimoni de marjades a la mediterrania occidental. una proposta de catalogacio. Technical report, Mallorca

Roger A (1997) *Court Traîté de Paysage.* Gallimard, Paris

Seva E, Román J, Seva R (2005) El origen prehistórico de los bancales/borda como habitación y refugio ganadero en la montaña de Alicante (España). *Mediterranea. Série de estudios biológicos* 18: 8–50

Telles G (1998) Paisagem global. In: Pinto-Correia T, Cancela de Abreu M (eds), *Challenges for Mediterranean landscape ecology: the future of cultural landscapes - examples from the Alentejo region: proceedings of the 1st national worshop of landscape ecology.* APEP - Portuguese Association for Landscape Ecology, Montemor-o-Novo

Varotto M (2008) Towards the rediscovery of the "middle landscapes". In: Scaramellini G, Varotto M (eds), *Terraced landscapes of the Alps.* Marsilio, Venice, 112–117

Villemus B (2004) Étude des murs de soutenement en maçonnerie et pierres seches. PhD Thesis, Institut National des Sciences Appliquées de Lyon. Université de Lyon

Watsuji T (2011) Fūdo, le milieu humain. CNRS, Paris. Originally published 1935

The Journal of ERSA
Powered by WU

ersa WU FWF

Volume 6, Number 1, 2019, 45–53
DOI: 10.18335/region.v6i1.262

journal homepage: region.ersa.org

The role of the European Union on immigration – An anthropological approach to the treaties that have been carried out in Europe in order to manage diversity

Carmen Clara Bravo Torres[1]

[1] Universidad de Granada, Granada, Spain

Received: 13 February 2019/Accepted: 10 July 2019

Abstract. Migrations are a global phenomenon that have prevailed throughout history. In recent decades there has been a need to control every person who enters and leaves the borders of a country. This fact can be observed in the European Union where in recent years the migratory phenomenon has appreciated as a problem. This institution carries out different measures in order to manage this diversity within its borders. However, these agreements are not adapted to the different contexts and are not carried out by all the countries that comprise this institution. In spite of all this, the discourse used by the European Union promotes the European identity in front of the rest, differentiating those considered others. These others are differentiated primarily by their nationality although from the discourse analysis, an economic factor can be observed. These themes will be studied in this paper, which will allow us to understand what treaties have been established in the European Union regarding migration and how diversity is managed from them.

Key words: European Union, Europeanization, Immigration and International Relations

1 Introduction

To understand this work, we should start from the idea that we are in a globalized world where transnational migrations are constant. These migrations have given rise to us being in a society characterized by the exchange of customs and languages. Depending on the context, we find different changes that have been of great importance for the case studied – the European Union. An example is Spain. This country has gone from being mainly a country that emits migrants, to being a recipient of a large number of people of different nationalities.

This situation has led to policies, laws, and different actions being challenged and reformulated to fit the current context but we should keep in mind that the migratory policies of a given country are governed by a series of norms and conventions that rule its usefulness. In the first place, it is important to highlight the competencies of the European Union, and then of the country studied. In this case, the Spanish Constitution, which is adapted to the European Union. Taking into account both aspects, we have in mind the International Treaties that the country has signed and ratified, then the laws or regulations with the rank of law and, finally, the regulations and collective agreements (as for example in the field of employment). Therefore, it is interesting to know what role this institution plays in the current migratory situation, with special emphasis on the processes of otherness that it manifests. A qualitative methodology has been carried out mainly for the accomplishment of this research, characterized by the bibliographical revision of experts both in migration issues and the role of the European Union in the international sphere. Among them, we highlight Barbé (2010, 2014), Olmos (2009) and Palomares Lerma (2010). It is necessary to be aware of the great dimension of the topics that are intended to be addressed in this document. Therefore, this work has been divided into a series of sections where different conventions have been treated in terms of policies of immigration, European councils, and the role of European identity over the rest. Treaties have been chosen since these are European mandates that have been determining the integration of the migrants in the European Union.

2   European immigration policies

Firstly, we must assume that the migration phenomenon is not a novel situation for the European Union. Migrations are a fundamental element of European identity. Since its formation, the European Union has been characterized by both emigration and immigration. Before the creation of the European Union, there already was a considerable flow of people between the different States, motivated primarily by the search for work (Cabré, Domingo 2002). From the Second World War, the need for labour increased. This led to the implementation of a series of measures to accommodate workers from other European States. This flow of people has been constant. Throughout history, some nationalities have predominated over others, since large numbers of people have been moving both within Europe and crossing their borders in times of economic recession and wars. At present, the migratory flow has been increasing, although a large number of people are not taken into account because the figures of migrants in Europe do not fit the reality.

While it is difficult to record all migratory flows, it should be noted that since the last century there is a greater need to restrict, control, and measure all issues that cross state borders, especially those that delimit the European Union (Moeykens 2013). An example of this is observed in Spain, when months before entering the European community the country was obliged to make the first regulation on the Rights and Duties of foreigners (Organic Law 7/1985, of July 1, on rights and freedoms of foreigners in Spain). From this moment, Spain has been influenced by the European Union and has a long legislative path around the migratory issue, since it is characterized by a constant change and a continuous redefinition. But do the laws agree with the existing reality? What is the purpose of these laws?

It is necessary to start from the idea that, as we will see later, in the development of the different Treaties that have tried to regulate immigration, the European Union is increasingly placing greater emphasis on immigration within its borders. This has been implemented since the Treaty of Lisbon, where the sovereignty of States has begun to be questioned as asylum or police cooperation have been regulated by the European Union. However, "many of the rules adopted in the field of immigration constitute what we call minimum standards, that is, they leave a wide margin of discretion to the States in terms of their development"[1] (Barbé 2010, p. 134). These policies appear in relation to the aspects of "integration" where the European Union has indicated what they refer to as good practices. These are a set of guidelines covering how States should act towards migrants entering the territory. However, these guidelines are very general and rarely followed in practice.

Three European states decided not to adjust to the regulation of migration imposed by the European Union. They carry out only those policies that interested him. These countries are Denmark, Ireland, and the United Kingdom (European Union 2015). From such distinctions we find how Europe does not present solid policies and is already divided

---

[1]Spanish original: "muchas de las normas que se adoptan en materia de inmigración constituyen lo que llamamos normas de contenido mínimo, es decir, que dejan un amplio margen de discrecionalidad a los Estados en cuanto a su desarrollo".

in different aspects. This challenges its representation as a unique institution. However, these general policies have been of great importance, especially those carried out with regard to border control, since the others have made it possible for the Member States to be more flexible in their implementation. Regarding border control, we should highlight the Schengen agreement, signed in 1985; which indicates the removal of internal borders. From this agreement, we can observe the relevance that the European Union to freedom of movement between certain countries. From this agreement, we can observe the relevance that the European Union brings to the freedom of movement between certain countries. In those cases where this free movement does not exist, it is necessary to emphasize the use of a visa, which will vary according to the country that you belong to and the stay in the determined country will require a series of permits. In the case of Spain, the residence permit and work permit for a certain economic amount are required, such as for researchers or "circular migrants" (migrant temporary workers). If they do not meet any of the requirements indicated for these types of migrations, their administrative status is considered irregular, despite spending time in Spain working and trying to legalize their situation. The only opportunity is to return to their country and from the so-called contingencies to be contracted by the State from the country of origin. From this fact, we can appreciate the importance of certain groups determined by their permission stay in a particular country.

In spite of the different policies established, which will be developed a posteriori, we must highlight that when there are laws specifically aimed at foreign people, such as immigration law, we are facing a situation where we differentiate us from the considered other. This influences which social policies get implemented. Not all policies are aimed at all people, only those that meet a number of conditions, such as the administrative situation of the subject in the host country. An example of this can be appreciated when, on 7 March 2016, the European Union entered into an agreement with Turkey where the expulsion of refugees from Europe is agreed, transferring them to Turkey, regardless of their country of origin.

From such policies, as here noted, we can see that the humanitarian character is not present in its measures since it is returning people fleeing for war reasons to another country. Although migration is considered as a right (Moeykens 2013), we find a large number of restrictions. In the case of the European Union, we observe how economic aspects have prevailed since its inception, relegating social aspects to a lower priority. For the European Union, what matters is the economy; it encourages external mobility but only to those within its borders. There is now a concern for the protection of the migrant, although this protection is based on the quest to obtain the maximum yield of these subjects. To this, it should be added that in the case of Spain the policies that are established are restorative since it has intervened when the error is already made and not preventive, as should be established. At present, we are dealing with this situation with regard to refugees, since the measures are being implemented based on the complex situation, without taking into account each individual who is being deported to another country. Situations like the one that is happening weaken the positioning of the European Union as an institution in the face of established international relations. A clear example is seen with refugees and since the wreck in Lampedusa. That is to say, "the prestige of the EU is partly conditioned by how it manages the challenge of migration. In this regard, the tragedy of the wreck in Lampedusa in October 2013 showed how far the EU is having instruments to respond effectively to irregular migration."[2] (Barbé 2014, p. 132).

Thus, we must take into account that we are faced with an institution based on economic aspects but whose reputation is influenced according to its management of different problems, as as the migratory flow. For this reason, in order to understand more clearly what role the European Union plays in immigration, in the following section we will analyse the treaties carried out since these set out the objectives of the European Union.

---

[2]Spanish original: "El prestigio de la UE está en parte condicionado por cómo gestiona el reto de la migración. En este sentido, la tragedia del naufragio en Lampedusa, en octubre de 2013, puso de manifiesto cuán lejos está la UE de disponer de unos instrumentos que le permitan responder de forma eficaz a la migración irregular."

2.1 Treaties by the European Union

This paper alludes to treaties from the area of justice, freedom, and security since it is the space that manages borders and mobility of citizens. Based on different treaties carried out in this area, the greater integration of States has been sought to participate as a single institution. However, the lack of consensus among countries has led to their role being questioned as a single institution in the international sphere. There are a number of challenges to the creation of a common migration policy since it is a policy shared among member states.

Firstly, in 1985, the need for free control of persons between the borders of the countries of the Member States was proclaimed, being a priority of cooperation in matters of justice, freedom, and security. The Schengen space was created but until 1995 it did not enter into force. Subsequently, in the Maastricht Treaty for the first time, reference is made to cooperation and the creation of an area of freedom, security, and justice. In addition, this treaty began to promote social aspects such as humanitarian aid. That is to say, "from Maastricht, all treaties reiterate that the EU will uphold and promote its values and interests, and it will contribute to the protection of its citizens, contribute to peace, security, sustainable development of the planet, solidarity and mutual respect among peoples, free trade and the eradication of poverty, the protection of human rights, respect for and development of international law and the principles of the Charter of the United Nations"[3] (Palomares Lerma 2010).

Nevertheless, we have to highlight to the Maastricht Treaty for its evolution of migration policies since this treaty was for intergovernmental cooperation but a posteriori this fact changed with the communitarization in all aspects except in the police and judicial cooperation in criminal matters (Barbé 2014).

Subsequent to this treaty we find the Treaty of Amsterdam, where "a very significant step was taken in integrating migration policy to the first community pillar; which allowed the extension of the ordinary legislative procedure in most matters, with the consequent participation of Parliament as co-legislator with the Council"[4] (Barbé 2014, p. 133). However, as explained above, the three aforementioned States decided to join only those measures that they considered appropriate. From that point on, the European Union had competence in terms of entry and residence, issuance of long-stay visas and residence permits; the residence of illegal immigrants, including repatriation and the conditions under which third-country nationals legally resident in one Member State may reside in another Member State.

Subsequent to this treaty, the current Treaty of Lisbon, "advocates the creation of a common migration policy. The Treaty led to the abolition of the system of pillars and the application of the ordinary legislative procedure in more areas of cooperation, including labour migration policy"[5] (Barbé 2014, p. 133). The Treaty sought the consolidation of a secure Union, tackling both issues of immigration as judicial cooperation and police (Palomares Lerma 2010). Since the Treaty of Lisbon, common visa policies and other residence permits have been adopted, such as controls at the external borders, elimination of controls irrespective of nationality within internal borders, fight against trafficking in human beings, repatriation issues, and exclusion. From the Lisbon Treaty onwards, "the Spanish Presidency of the European Union during the first half of 2010 set out the following objectives in the area of external action: Consolidating a Safer Union for its citizens, tackling together the challenge of Immigration and building a shared space for judicial and police cooperation"[6] (Palomares Lerma 2010).

---

[3]Spanish original: "Desde Maastricht, todos los tratados reiteran que la UE afirmará y promoverá sus valores e intereses y contribuirá a la protección de sus ciudadanos, contribuirá a la paz, seguridad, desarrollo sostenible del planeta, solidaridad y respeto mutuo entre los pueblos, el libre comercio y justo, la erradicación de la pobreza, la protección de los derechos humanos, el respeto y desarrollo del Derecho Internacional y los principios de la Carta de Naciones Unidas".

[4]Spanish original: "se dio un paso muy significativo al integrarse la política de migración al primer pilar comunitario; lo cual permitió la extensión del procedimiento legislativo ordinario en la mayoría de materias, con la consiguiente participación del Parlamento como colegislador junto al Consejo"

[5]Spanish original: "aboga por la creación de una política de migración común. El Tratado condujo a la abolición del sistema de pilares y la aplicación del procedimiento legislativo ordinario en más áreas de cooperación, incluyendo la política de migración laboral".

[6]Spanish original: "La presidencia española de la Unión Europea durante el primer semestre de 2010

In addition to the different treaties carried out, agreements and conventions have been enacted regarding the management of the migratory flow. Among them is the Dublin Convention. Based on this agreement, it established that each member country is responsible for managing and studying the different asylum applications. This is done so that there is only one request and it will not be in the country of preference. It can be requested in the country where you have relatives or in the country of arrival. This agreement was signed in 1990 and subsequently ratified by its member states. It was updated in 2003 and in 2013. At present this agreement is not working since the main weight falls on the countries of entry; therefore, the situation is disproportionate. Just as refugee rights are currently being violated since the established laws are not being carried out, mainly only the country of arrival is being taken into account, and family ties and accepted requests are not taken into account. The European Union is failing in this aspect and should look for proposals and alternatives to correct the bad management of the migratory flows that it is carrying out. Besides, it should be noted that with the approval of convention Stockholm (2009) immigration and asylum policies are strengthened towards neighbouring countries.

Additionally, in terms of integration, a number of multi-annual programs have been carried out through European Councils that set targets over a period of five years, as the Treaties provide for little regulation (Barbé 2014). For this research we have studied the Councils in recent years, from 2009 to 2017. We have studied the number of councils where the European Union talked about the migrations, in what way, and what perception reflects the different subjects. This last aspect will be developed in the next section where we will show the image that the European Union transmits of immigrants, migrants, and refugees.

During these six years, 25 councils have mentioned the migratory phenomenon. At some periods, the topic was barely touched, at others it was the focus of the councils. In 2010 and 2011, all the councils talk about the migratory phenomenon. In these years, the importance of the integration of irregular immigrants is pointed out. In addition, these councils emphasize the importance of foreign relations. Events in the Mediterranean and in Libya stand out. In 2013 and 2014, the councils talked about the need for jobs for immigrants, without specifying their administrative situation in the country of arrival. They also highlight the importance of external relations to control and manage borders. In 2015, these councils emphasized the fight against terrorism, stressing the importance of border control. This last year, all the councils made mention of the migratory phenomenon, emphasizing the cooperation between the different countries and the European Union. They also highlight the need for counter-terrorism and the need to prevent illegal immigration. Thus, based on the analysis of these councils, there is talk of integration, but they do not indicate measures to achieve it. They focus on controlling, managing, and monitoring all those who cross European borders, with the aim of economic profitability, since the emphasis is only on integration from employment. In the Europe 2020 strategy, with regard to European policies, the immigrant only appears once, and in the Green Paper emphasis is placed on labour immigration and strategies are sought for maximum economic gains, in addition to the facilities that are given to circular immigrants.

Therefore, we can observe the importance given to the economic aspects of immigration policies, as it looks at their control and profitability, instead of taking into account other essential factors such as the need for immigrants with respect to the aging of the population. But as we can see through circular migrations, not only do European policies play an important role in migration, but the countries that sign agreements with the European Union facilitate the movement of these people. This can be seen from the acceptance of Turkey regarding the reception of immigrants. It is therefore interesting to consider which aspects are taken into account in neighbourhood policies. In line with the idea proposed by the European Union, it is necessary to cooperate with the country of origin in migration policies, as this will lead to better management.

---

planteó los siguientes objetivos en el ámbito de la acción exterior: Consolidar una Unión más segura para sus ciudadanos, afrontando conjuntamente el reto de la inmigración y construyendo un espacio compartido de cooperación judicial y policial".

Firstly, we must point out that border management in the European Union is managed by FRONTEX (European Agency for Operational Cooperation at the External Borders of the member states of the European Union) and the corresponding border guard services in third countries. Despite the designation of this border, account should be taken of the policies entered into with these third countries and that "the European Union has chosen its proximity countries, since it is these countries that generate more migration flows into the Union"[7] (Barbé 2014, p. 132). But in order to be able to understand the neighbourhood policies that are carried out, we should take into account the designations that are used to name the subjects. For this reason, the next section will analyze how, based on what was studied, the subjects studied are designated and constructed as different, in order to deepen the neighbourhood policies in the future. These policies have benefits in terms of economic, social, political, and cultural aspects. Primarily they are based on the strategic associations in search of greater economic growth in both countries.

2.2 Regular immigration / irregular immigration / asylum

Designations for naming a subject have great relevance for the group that represents him as the represented, since "the denominations represent the most primary form of description. So that the simple fact of 'how to call' things, people, or phenomena can help the treatment they receive"[8] (Olmos 2009, p. 245). Thus, from the denominations we represent the rest of the population by which we establish differences with those that we consider the "others" different from "we". This fact we observe in speeches and in laws and regulations at state level. Common examples include the denomination of immigrant, illegal or irregular immigrant, foreigner, or refugee. "The creation of a new legal instrument on immigration leads to the emergence of new categories of subjects; To foreign / national distinction, is added from European foreign / non-EU immigrants and within the latter establishes an even lower, illegal or irregular classification."[9] (Briceño 2004, p. 205).

The terms mentioned play a fundamental role in the naming of others, so they must be explained in detail. But, it is necessary to start from the difference of foreigner / immigrant. A foreigner is one who does not have Spanish nationality. However, immigrants are the majority, if characterized by a relative change of residence in a given time (Castelo 2005). Therefore, no human being is illegal or legal, but its administrative situation in the country of origin may be regulated or not.

With regard to irregular immigration, the European Union has given it great importance as there is an interest in fighting illegal immigration because they are perceived in a negative way. These subjects are constructed as an other different from us, to distance ourselves even more from them and to justify the measures taken. That is why border management and the different preventive measures are important since most of the collaboration with countries neighbouring have been to reduce clandestine immigration flows. It is important to highlight how readmission agreements have been implemented: "The readmission agreements are formally international agreements signed by the European Union and a third State. It is an agreement with a highly technical content that specifies the assumptions and procedures under which the readmission of an irregular immigrant in his country of origin is foreseen."[10] (Barbé 2010, p. 136). Although these readmissions are a fundamental right.

---

[7]Spanish original: "la UE ha optado por los países de su proximidad, dado que son estos países los que generan más flujos migratorios hacia la Unión".

[8]Spanish original: "las normalizaciones/denominaciones suponen la forma más primaria de descripción, de tal manera que el simple hecho de 'cómo llamar' a las cosas, personas o fenómenos ... puede ayudar al trato que reciben".

[9]Spanish original: "De la creación de un nuevo instrumento jurídico en materia de inmigración se deriva la emergencia de nuevas categorías de sujeto; a la distinción extranjero/nacional, se añade de extranjero europeo/ inmigrantes no comunitarios y dentro de esta última se establece una clasificación aun inferior, ilegal o irregular".

[10]Spanish original: "Los acuerdos de readmisión son formalmente acuerdos internacionales firmados por la Unión Europea y un tercer Estado. Se trata de un acuerdo con un contenido altamente técnico en el que se especifican los supuestos y procedimientos bajo los cuales se prevé la readmisión de un inmigrante irregular en su país de origen."

This is a very costly situation, so the European Union has promoted specific incentives, such as the facilitation of obtaining visas. This is a step towards the liberalization of visas. However, these measures are not taken together with the countries closest to Spain in the Mediterranean neighbourhood. We can therefore highlight how, in the area of irregular immigration, the European Union has agreements with certain countries for readmission, but based on clearly Europeanising measures linked to security (Barbé 2010).

With regard to regular migration, it should be noted that it is not a global priority for the European Union. However, it does play an important role in terms of employment since different agreements are in place to allow regular migration. "It is important to note that bilateral cooperation has been developed between some Member States of the European Union and Morocco in order to strengthen the temporary recruitment of Moroccan nationals in EU countries"[11] (Barbé 2010, p. 142). This fact can also be seen with the creation of the Green Paper, which focuses on labour migration and economic migration. For this reason, workers are differentiated between skilled workers, seasonal workers, paid interns, self-employed, and workers transferred by multinationals (Bazzaco 2008). However, the European Union does not focus on those migrants whose administrative situation in the country is not regulated.

Unlike the two aspects mentioned above, cooperation in the field of asylum between European Union and other countries has been based on the protection of refugees from the 1951 Geneva Convention on the Status of Refugees. This Convention not only takes into account refugees, but also those who, despite not being refugee, are at risk of persecution in their country. According to Barbé (2014), one of the key elements established in this Geneva regime was the principle of non-refoulement. But this seems not to be very clear since in the case of Turkey and Syria, we are witnessing this principle not being fulfilled. To these breaches must be added the lack of coherence and agreement between the different countries of the European Union with its neighbours since contexts of this institution are different and each of them has interests and opposing thoughts regarding policies established with neighbouring countries.

So that, "in an increasingly interdependent world, the European Union is working for economic and commercial globalization, which will benefit everyone, as well as the search for political stability in the world. By carrying out cooperation and assistance, the Union contributes to the achievement of the objectives of peace, development and security for all. It is necessary to remember that we are in a multipolar world and that, under these circumstances of international society, the states of the European Union can only defend their values, objectives and interests if they speak with one voice in the world"[12] (Palomares Lerma 2010, p. 20).

But each context is unique and there is no clear consensus among different states to represent as a single institution. This can lead to great havoc at the social level. However, they are all represented as Europe, with a common identity which they want to claim.

3   Europe and the Others

This Europeanization is represented in the established policies and in the catalogues of each one of the individuals. Therefore, it is necessary to emphasize that "we believe that to identify, to call, to denominate to some people 'immigrants' and other 'foreigners' influences in the way in which we perceive them because one designation and another they have loads of different values"[13] (Olmos 2009, p. 71). Thus, foreigner does not

---

[11]Spanish original: "Es importante destacar que se ha venido desarrollando cooperación bilateral entre algunos Estados Miembros de la Unión Europea y Marruecos a fin de fortalecer el reclutamiento con carácter temporal de nacionales marroquís en países de la U.E.".

[12]Spanish original: "En un mundo cada vez más interdependiente, la UE trabaja por una globalización económica y comercial más justa, que redunde en beneficio de todos, y también en la búsqueda de estabilidad política en el mundo. Realizando labores de cooperación y ayuda, la Unión contribuye a alcanzar los objetivos de paz, desarrollo y seguridad para todos. Es necesario recordar que nos encontramos en un mundo multipolar y que, bajo estas circunstancias de la sociedad internacional, los Estados de la Unión Europea sólo pueden defender sus valores, objetivos e intereses si hablan con una sola voz en el mundo"

[13]Spanish original: "creemos que identificar, llamar, denominar a algunas personas 'inmigrantes' y a otras 'extranjeros' influye en la forma en que las percibimos porque una designación y otra tienen cargas

have the same meaning as immigrant since foreigner refers to both those who comply with the regulations established in the laws of foreigners, as well as those belonging to the European Union and those who have a specific economic rent. The established discourse is of great relevance since from the term that we use to denominate the people we are associating the group with different visions of ethnic elements, motivations, and determined opportunities (García et al. 2008). We are in a country belonging to the European Community where concrete policies are attributed similar to the rest of this community, even though the contexts are totally different. These policies influence the public discourse both outside and within the system. Therefore, this fact has relevant consequences at the social level.

Regarding terminology, it is important to note that despite of the many different words and policies that are used for people who arrive in Spain, those who leave the country are all referred to as 'emigrants'. This is regardless of whether their destination is inside or outside of the European Union, and regardless of the administrative situation of the country. Through this, we appreciate how the legislation itself shows the importance of being considered European, discriminating and considering different people who do not belong to that community. Therefore, "It is necessary to understand the migratory policy in Spain as a consequence of the European dictates, under the ideology of the construction of the "Fortress Europe", which explains many of the contradictory discourses and policy reactions developed in this country" (Agrela, Gil 2004, p. 6). Continuing with the Spanish context and with most European countries; we are faced with dynamic contexts, which are not taken into account in many of the policies or in the social discourse because subjects are categorized for ethnic elements, irrespective of their position in the European country studied. This fact is observed with young people called second generation (Barquín 2009, Massot 2005, Moreno 2002). All these attributions can have great consequences in the collective social imaginary as in the identity of each of the subjects. Therefore, the policies put in place by the European Union and the terminology used can contribute significantly to the construction of the other, thus reinforcing the European identity. Thus, it should be emphasized that this identity, like any process of otherness and identification, arises from essentialist categories typical of a Eurocentric view.

4   Final Reflections

The migration phenomenon has always been an issue that has been present in the European Union. However, currently immigration has been problematized and this institution is not able to cope with this flow of people as it does not present a clear and real distinction in terms of the legislative figure represented by the different subjects. That is, it is clear who is a foreigner and a community citizen, but there is no distinction between immigrant and refugee. However, in treaties and agreements a differentiation is established, although not clear, since they mention that said measures are aimed at a specific group, such as refugees. From the established treaties, the right to emigrate, solidarity, and the management and importance of asylum applications stand out. However, we find that it is not being fulfilled and at present, the European Union does not have a common asylum or immigration policy. Only a series of agreements with different countries are established. These are scarce and do not cover the existing problems.

The current policies are restrictive and are based on border control, promoting differentiation with respect to the "others". Although such differences will vary according to the country and the framed categories, mainly based on ethnic and economic reasons. These are justified by the administrative situation in the country of destination. With regard to irregular immigration, the European Union focuses on Europeanization, while regular immigration is based on rules and agreements between different countries. As far as asylum applications are concerned, they prevail in international standards that although in spite of being scarce, are not being met.

From the analysis of the treaties, agreements, and advice made, the need to control borders, the externalization of resources with respect to the management of migratory flows, and the criminalization granted to some people is observed. The measures that

---

de valores distintos".

the European Union is carrying out, the political discourse, and the role of the media
have great importance because it is not having a humanitarian character in this situation,
producing a boom in political parties of far right where the racism and the nationalism
are encouraged. We must be aware of the current situation of the European Union and of
the influence that its actions have at a social level.

References

Agrela B, Gil S (2004) Constructing Otherness. The Management of migration and diversity in the Spanish context. *Migration: European Journal of International Migration and Ethnic Relations* 43

Barbé E (2010) *La Unión Europea más allá de sus fronteras. ¿Hacia la transformación del Mediterráneo y Europa Oriental?* Tecnos, Madrid

Barbé E (2014) *La Unión Europea en las Relaciones Internacionales.* Tecnos, Madrid

Barquín A (2009) ¿De dónde son los hijos de los inmigrantes? La construcción de la identidad y la escuela. *Educar* 44: 81–96

Bazzaco E (2008) La Unión Europea frente a los procesos migratorios: lejos de una política integral. *Papers* 104: 57–65

Briceño Y (2004) Inmigración, exclusión y construcción de la alteridad. La figura del inmigrante en el contexto español. In: Mato D (ed), *Políticas de ciudadanía y sociedad civil en tiempos de globalización.* faces, Universidad de Venezuela, Caracas

Cabré A, Domingo A (2002) Flujos migratorios hacia Europa: actualidad y perspectivas. *Arbor* 172: 325–344. CrossRef.

Castelo G (2005) Logros y Retos del frente Indígena Oaxaqueño Binacional: una organización para el futuro de los migrantes indígenas. Tesis licenciatura. universidad de las américas públicas

European Union (2015) European Union Law: Justice, freedom and security. https://eur-lex.europa.eu/summary/chapter/justice_freedom_security.html?root_default=SUM_1_CODED%3D23

García FJ, Rubio M, Bouachra O (2008) Población inmigrante en y escuela en España: Un balance de investigación. *Revista de educación* 345: 23–60

Massot I (2005) Hijas e hijos de inmigrantes: la mal llamada segunda generación. *Abaco: Revista de cultura y ciencias sociales* 43: 67–78

Moeykens E (2013) El derecho a migrar como un Derecho Universal: los derechos del migrante en el Estado democrático de Derecho. X Jornadas de Sociología. Facultad de Ciencias Sociales. Universidad de Buenos Aires, Buenos Aires

Moreno P (2002) Reflexiones en torno a la segunda generación de inmigrantes y la construcción de la identidad. *Ofrim suplementos* 10: 9–30

Olmos A (2009) La población inmigrante extranjera y la construcción de la diferencia. Discursos de alteridad en el sistema educativo andaluz. Doctoral thesis. Universidad de Granada

Palomares Lerma G (2010) La Unión Europea en la sociedad internacional. In: Estudios de Política Exterior (ed), *Cuadernos pedagógicos sobre la Unión Europea. La acción exterior de la Unión Europea.* Estudios de Política Exterior, Madrid, 3–16

REGION

The Journal of ERSA
Powered by WU

Volume 5, Number 3, 2018, 21–38
DOI: 10.18335/region.v5i3.204

journal homepage: region.ersa.org

The Mediterranean Variety of Capitalism, Flexibility of Work Schedules, and Labour Productivity in Southern Europe

Alberto Vallejo-Peña[1], Sandro Giachi[2]

[1] Universidad de Málaga, Málaga, Spain
[2] University of Sussex, Brighton, United Kingdom

Received: 13 September 2017/Accepted: 23 August 2018

Abstract. Sociology has long been used to highlight the existence of diverse institutional models between geographical areas of Europe in terms of work organization. Based on this, we propose to compare the situation of four representative countries of Southern Europe (Spain, Italy, Greece and Portugal) with that of the rest of Europe, by addressing the number of hours worked and the flexibility of working hours as key elements of their institutional model of work organization, as well as their impact on levels of labour productivity. Taking the model of the varieties of capitalism as a reference, this study compares the behaviour of the Mediterranean (Southern) countries with other European regions. Indicators have been obtained from the 2010 and 2015 iterations of the European Working Conditions Survey (EWCS) that include the number of hours worked, the flexibility in the hours of entry and exit, and the tendency to work the same number of hours per day. After comparing averages in both iterations and applying linear regressions, the following conclusions have been reached: (1) Productivity in Southern countries is on a par with the European average but far from the more corporatist and liberal (northern) areas; (2) the South maintains a high average of hours worked (above the European average) to compensate for the poor productivity of its hours; and (3) the incorporation of flexible schedules is associated with elevated levels of productivity.

JEL classification: J81, P52, B52

Key words: Economies of Southern Europe, European crisis, PIGS, Varieties of capitalism

1 Introduction

The development of the political, economic, and social project of the European Union (EU) recently highlighted the historical heterogeneity of Europe. Indeed, from an external point of view, Europe may be something more than a continent: it is a geographical area united by its history, the core territory for the development of the Western society that generated this political, cultural, and economic phenomenon called Eurocentrism (Brennetot et al. 2013). However, such a model gradually declined in front of emergent regions such as the United States (U.S.) since the beginning of the 20th century, and

South-Eastern Asia during the last three decades (Lamo de Espinosa 2010). To what degree has the heterogeneity of Europe contributed to its current situation? Despite the difficulty in responding to such a question, our work looks at some key elements of national organizational cultures. Among the evident economic and cultural differences existing within Europe, we highlight those that – in our opinion – have led to the Southern European countries ('the South') being labelled as a threat to the stability of the European Union. These refer to a specific historical cycle: countries like Spain and Portugal maintained their historical weight during their colonial period, after completing their 'brilliant' cycle during the age of discoveries and mercantilism. Likewise, Italy was a very relevant node for the international economy and commerce between the 14th and the 16th centuries. Afterwards, the Industrial Revolution was a key stage that turned the situation around and favoured Northern countries.

More recently, Spain, Italy, Greece, and Portugal joined the European Union in evident conditions of backwardness when compared with their Northern partners. Nevertheless, the growth of the Italian economy during the 1980s led to its Gross Domestic Product (GDP) per capita being on a par with that of the United Kingdom (U.K.) at various times during that decade. Furthermore, the significant economic growth of Spain between the 1990s and the beginning of the 21st century, suggested that the "European dream" of equilibrating the North-South balance was an achievable goal. By contrast, the fall of both countries (Italy and Spain) after the "Lehmann Brothers" crash in 2008 suggested that the period of prosperity of previous years was based on a temporary favourable situation, betraying – in turn – their shortcomings in terms of innovation, technology, industrialization, and creation of employment. Likewise, Portugal and Greece recently experienced a gradual deterioration in their economies. The Greek situation was particularly critical, due to the country's indebtedness and the consequent threat to the eurozone.[1]

Regarding the labour performance of Southern European countries, evidence corroborates some weaknesses when compared with the North. Portugal and Greece show concerning outcomes in terms of productivity per worked hour: 100 being the average of EU-28, they score 70.1 and 70.6 respectively, while Italy (101.7) and Spain (101.1) are closer to the average. But all these countries are far from the scores of their Northern partners such as Belgium (134.7), the Netherlands (129.5), France (128.0) and Germany (127.0). A report by the McKinsey Global Institute (MGI 2010), assigning 100 points to the current level of labour productivity of the U.S., gives 84 points to Northern Europe, and 73 points to Southern European countries. The report concludes as follows: while the productivity of Europe was closer to the U.S. during the 90s, since the beginning of the new century it continues to decrease, burdened by Southern countries that have embarked on a 'non-sustainable' path.

In addition, the elevated public deficit of the South has led to a conflict with their European partners that are not impressed with the South's governance and economic performance. The most significant criticisms include the following examples: the trend toward the waste of public money, "clientelism", management inefficiencies, overweight of the public administration sector, and – above all – the poor levels of labour productivity. A prominent Spanish sociologist, Lamo de Espinosa (2010, p. 543) affirmed that: "This situation provoked serious concerns about the solidity and the potential of the Spanish economy and, to a lesser extent, about the reaction capacity of both its institutions and political elite. International press condemned Spain to the fellowship of the PIGS (Portugal, Italy, Greece, Spain): a stigma that will last for a long time." (Translation provided by the authors)

Scholars have often recognized that these inequalities rely on the existence of a gap in

---

[1] Given the difficulties of financing manifested by Southern European countries and their incapability of generating sustainable economic growth, some Northern partners and institutions reported such situation as a waste of their financial contributions to the Union. Did the South create a 'subvention culture'? Public aid to peripheral and convergence regions – justified by rebalancing goals – ended with a positive, but temporary and fictitious effect that dwindled out as aid reduced over time (De la Fuente 2005). More pessimistic scholars have suggested that aid from the European Union to underdeveloped regions had almost no effect on rebalancing structural gaps between Northern and Southern countries in terms of employment, innovation, industry fabric, and technology (González Rodríguez et al. 2000).

terms of production and the occupational model. For instance, Miguélez, Prieto (2009) focused on the construction of an unbalanced labour model diminishing the value of the working class. While Northern Europe consolidated a stable model for employment during the 1950-80 period, "Southern European countries were left behind because of the concentration of low-quality employment and the low levels of inclusion of women in the labour market". Miguélez, Prieto (2009, p. 276; translation provided by the authors) In addition, since the 80s, this framework was subsequently weakened by new factors that jeopardize social rights: "First of all, the strength of the system of labour relations of each country; and then, the inclusion within the employment system of new labour actors that are different from the adult white male, such as the youth, women, and immigrants. [...] In countries like Spain the dualism of the labour model is clearly evident." (Miguélez, Prieto 2009, p. 276; translation provided by the authors)

Regarding the recent application of governmental policies that promote productivity in Southern Europe, we observed two main lines of action: policies to reduce working time and those aimed at flexicurity. Regarding the first case, the promotion of low-wage policies in the European Union since the early 2000s stands out. Its applications, both in the North and in the South, do not work properly, at least from a productivity perspective (Perrons 2005). The model of contracting workers for short periods with low wages is compensated with the incentive of occupying the rest of the day with other dedications and even a second job, in addition to having tax benefits and exemption from Social Security. However, the subsequent results – both in the north and in the south – showed some reinforcement of situations of poverty, lack of worker motivation and feminization of these contracts, which reinforced the figure of the male breadwinner. Among the forms adopted in Europe, the consolidation of the German mini-job model stands out, by finding the right context for its development, as Feld et al. (2015) indicated in a recent work. According to them, "many of those with a mini-job are second earners, students and pensioners [...] and compared to other European countries, Germany's support system is rather generous" (Feld et al. 2015, p. 3). Given those circumstances, to export such a model successfully to Southern countries shows several difficulties. In terms of policies aimed at flexicurity, expectations are somewhat more optimistic. In a study conducted by a mixed team of Spanish and Italian researchers, they focused on the following question: is flexicurity exportable (Leonardi et al. 2011)? Although Italy and Spain are labour markets that are traditionally rigid and conditioned by cultural factors, some steps have been taken in this direction through dialogue between social actors, and there is considerable room for improvement if the work training is adapted to the new times and the mediation between supply and demand.

With these relevant policy issues in mind, we expose in this paper the outcomes of our research into the differences of labour productivity and national models of work organization between culturally and historically similar Southern European countries (Italy, Spain, Portugal, and Greece) and the rest of the EU, giving special attention to Northern countries. We used data from the fifth (2010) and sixth (2015) iterations of the European Working Conditions Survey (EWCS) performed by the European Foundation for the Improvement of Living and Working Conditions (EUROFOUND), located in Dublin, Ireland. We identified a number of measures relating to the flexibility of working schedules as indicators of national organizational models. The second section details the theoretical framework; the third section describes research goals, design, and methodology; the fourth section shows the findings, while the last section details the conclusion of this study.

2 Varieties of capitalism, work organization, and time management

The starting point of our research is the assumption that the national context affects economic factors like organizational and work practices. The influence of the work of Inglehart (1997), who oriented his studies toward the value of interculturalism and toward cross-country differences, was crucial for studying national cultures. Likewise, we should highlight the research performed by Esping-Andersen (1999), connecting national cultures with the socio-political context. This scholar identified three models of development of the welfare state across western countries since the end of World War II: liberal, conservative, and social democratic. Beyond the public sector, every (public or private) organization is embedded within such models.

Likewise, we should take into account the contributions from the neo-institutionalist research approach. Mauro Guillén (1994), the author of 'Models of Management', tackles such differences according to the economic and labour relations existing internally in each country. The thesis that the traditions of different countries mark their institutional relations and shared ideology is useful in explaining most of the existing organizational and labour conflicts, thereby generating a diversified set of paradigms. For example, it is part of the stream that underlies contrasting conceptual axes such as 'Catholic versus Protestant' or 'liberal versus conservative'. In each country, we find institutional struggles that determine the dominance of a certain paradigm. This approach helps us to understand the different organizational models existing across countries and nations. Specifically, we state that a neo-institutional approach is useful for addressing the socio-political diversity of European countries and its impact on labour productivity. Some empirical studies have included a similar approach, like the global comparative exercise performed by Hall, Jones (1996); the comparative studies about Canadian regions performed by Baldwin et al. (2005) and Maynard (2007) and the analysis of the Spanish economy coordinated by Segura (2006). Such approximations show that institutional relations encompass one of the most relevant components of a national economy in facilitating labour productivity, technological capacity, workforce qualification and internationalization. Therefore, we find several studies connecting labour productivity with the existence of values, norms, and rules (the institutional framework) facilitating the flexibility of the labour system and the cultural value of work organization.

Within the neo-institutional literature, a relevant contribution is provided by the 'varieties of capitalism' literature (Hall, Soskice 2001). These studies highlighted the relevance of national institutions within the economic structure, using conditioning variables such as innovation and performance. The varieties of capitalist models across countries and territories have historical reasons and imply different values and beliefs. The institutional effect primarily manifests itself in the governance mechanisms of industrial relations. These factors condition the capacity of nations (and their firms) to adapt to the challenges posed by globalization and the emergence of the knowledge economy (Castells 1997, Hall, Soskice 2001). Organizational flexibility of markets and firms (e.g. through new models of labour relations or network organizations) stands out as a key factor to foster firms' productivity and competitiveness.

This approach recognizes the existence of different ideal types of organization for the capitalist economy in Europe (Crouch 1998). For instance, some studies highlight the existence of a 'Mediterranean' model of capitalism for countries such as Italy, Spain, Portugal, and Greece (Amable 2003). The idea of a Mediterranean model of capitalism takes its origin from the existence of a large set of family-based small firms, cross-participation in firms' governance and the prominent role of the State in the economy (Moerland 1995, Regini 1995), a system that De Jong (1995, p. 402) defined as a 'pragmatic' one. According to Amable (2003), this variety of capitalism is significantly different to the liberal (or Anglo-Saxon) model that is based on the balance between the limiting and creative effect of institutions on the economy through formal regulation mechanisms. Moreover, some countries of central Europe (e.g. Germany) adopt a 'corporatist' market economy, while Scandinavian countries adopt a social-democratic model (Amable 2003). These models, especially the latter, stand out for their level of long-range planning on national public policies while, at the same time, firms' recruitment strategies do not necessarily rely on close social networks. As Cassano (1996) points out, there are historical and cultural reasons explaining why Mediterranean countries developed a peculiar way of understanding organization, work, and time.

Specifically, the Mediterranean model of capitalism "is similar to the Continental European model, but based on more employment protection and less social protection. Employment protection is made possible by a relatively low level of product-market competition and the absence of short-term profit constraints as a consequence of the centralization of the financial system. However, a workforce with limited skills and education level does not allow for the implementation of high wages and high skills industrial strategy" (Amable 2009, p. 21), while "Mediterranean countries appear to possess more regulated labour markets than other European economies" (Amable 2003, p. 17). Therefore, the Mediterranean model is more rigid than others are in terms of governance and organization of employment. Formal employment protection prevents quick structural change, while low competitive pressure simultaneously allows employment stability in large firms. This situation also hinders the need for upgrading the competences of the workforce and, therefore, potential pathways for innovation and productivity (Amable 2003, p. 113).[2]

In conclusion, (Amable 2003, 2009) suggested that the rigidity of the labour market in Southern European countries seriously hinders the capacity of their firms to compete and, therefore, he recommended exploring more 'flexible' forms of governance and organization of work. However, as Meardi (2012, p. 58-59) pointed out, this supposed 'rigidity' of Mediterranean countries should be considered according to some dimensions and not others: for instance, Spain (and Portugal) showed very high levels of temporary work for a very long period, in contrast with the situation of Italy and Greece. This difference originated in the different degrees of conflict in industrial relations and strength of unionism. By contrast, rigidity looks to be a common feature of all Mediterranean countries as it comes to the daily organization of work, as it can be exemplified by the rigidity of the working-time schedules.

Drawing from the considerations above mentioned, our research hypothesis is the following: the Mediterranean model of capitalism is less productive because of the low flexibility of the organization of working time and schedules, among other factors. Alongside the theoretical contributions exposed above, there is evidence of significant differences in work schedules between Northern and Southern European countries. For instance, it is well-known that workdays in the north used to end relatively early (usually around 18:00 hours) versus the extensive working evening typical of Mediterranean private firms. In this sense, the work gets more centrality in Southern countries' work schedules. Among the explanations for the overloading of working time we highlight the studies of Paugam (2007) and Halbwachs (2002). They recognize the difficulty of Southern societies in separating working time from private or social time. They also found a historical trend within Southern countries to split the workday in two. This probably derives from diverse factors like climate or the 'moonlighting' tradition that evolved as a consequence of recurrent famines (i.e. an additional evening job to compensate for the difficulties in obtaining income). The 'classic' works of the German sociologist Georg Simmel (1998) went further in its implications by placing Southern Europe as an example of 'integrated poverty': a situation addressing a large part of the population, contagious and reproductive in nature, and weakened by a strong component of "clientelism" and informal economy. Simmel identified family solidarity as the solution adopted by the lower classes for addressing this problem in Mediterranean countries. Familism and 'clan culture' (Banfield 1958, Pizzorno 1966, López-Pintor, Wert 1982) contribute to impeding the separation between work and private space and time. In conclusion, this complex convergence of diverse factors provoked a specific model of adaptation that is no longer relevant to current societies and economies, thereby causing a societal disorder of work organization.

This tendency towards work time overloading worsened after the Great Recession of 2008 with its consequent social cuts to public expenditure in Greece, Spain, and Portugal, causing a fall of salaries and an unbalanced context for negotiation between workers and private firms. Additional problems came from the increase of mandatory working hours in the public sector in these countries that, likewise, reduced the number of temporary workers employed by the public administration.

On the other hand, the low productivity of the countries of the south is also explicable by political science, focusing on the forms of government. In this sense, Migdal (1998) developed his perspective "State in society" that conceives the State as an area of

---

[2]Another key feature of the Mediterranean model is specialization in light industries and low-tech activities, as well as heavy product-market regulation, hindering technological innovation and entrepreneurship – as confirmed by the lagging position that Southern European countries have in terms of ICTs (Amable 2003, ch. 1).

power marked by the use of force, and where the legal and institutional framework is complemented by informal processes and power relations. The State is not only influenced by international and global issues, but also – to a large extent – by social and ideological interests of a local or regional nature. In this same line, the perspective of "neopatrimonialism" helps to explain the dysfunctions of many governments of the planet. The classic work of Bratton, Van de Walle (1997), Democratic experiences in Africa (see also Van de Walle 2005), speaks of a strong transmission of the interests of certain social groups toward government mechanisms that prevented genuine development of democracy. The authors identify as characteristics of a "neopatrimonialist" government: (1) "presidentialism", understood as the concentration of power in a few hands; (2) "clientelism"; and (3) The use of state resources for private interests. Approaching the case of Latin American governments, Bechle (2010) explains that society has not found a way to control political power, since it operates continuously crossing the border between public and private. Weber, according to Bechle, predicted that a patrimonial stage in the governments would give way to the domain of the legal system, but this phase has been completed by a select group of countries (Northern Europe being a reference). In the Latin American case, however, there is a particular context in which private interests and patrimonial forms continue to be active, under the cover of legality. Maya (2016) has reinforced these arguments in her recent work on the decline of "Chavism" in Venezuela. In this sense, the southern European countries correspond to the model only partially, but the theory warns of the existence of strong patronage networks in the environment of their governments (Villena 2017).

Among the most relevant strategies promoted by the policy and management sector to foster labour productivity through a change in the working-time system are those strategies based on time flexibilization. There are two types of initiatives: on the one hand, the so-called passive flexibility (1) that enables the firm to adapt work schedules to workers' demands and needs by offering benefits like free days or salary incentives (Lusa, et 2007); or on the other hand, flexibility policies oriented to the personnel (2) fostering its satisfaction and motivation through improvement in work-family conciliation (Jijena-Michel, Jijena-Michel 2015, Lewis 2003). In both cases, and especially (2), the support perceived by the worker may be translated into positive attitudes with significant impacts on productivity, according to both Perceived Organizational Support Theory and Social Exchange theories (Lambert 2000). In this sense, earlier policies of flexibilization oriented toward the 'when' of the problem, were integrated with others oriented toward the 'where' and the 'to what extent' (Hill et al. 2008). In fact, recent empirical studies show that modifying the working schedule system of firms could improve both family-work conciliation and labour productivity (Basque Governement 2010).

3 Methodology

The aim of this research is to measure the flexibility of work schedules and its impact on labour productivity across Southern European countries by performing a comparison with three other areas previously defined by theory (varieties of capitalism approach). To achieve this aim, we designed a comparative and exploratory study. Our research used data from all EU-28 countries for theoretical and operational reasons (we use the average of European countries as a reference) even if our research design is focused on comparing the performance of the following four blocs of countries:[3]

---

[3]We excluded from this classification smaller countries (like Cyprus, Luxembourg, or Malta) because their institutional model is not clearly positioned according to the literature. For instance, it is not clear if Cyprus should be considered as a case of the liberal variety of capitalism, or mixed/Mediterranean. Likewise, the disproportionate levels of labour productivity exhibited by Luxembourg, probably due to its peculiar economic structure (e.g. international finance), prompted the exclusion of this country from the classification. Furthermore, almost all of the countries corresponding to the central or eastern part of Europe (following the United Nations's scheme) were not included in any bloc as most of them would correspond to the post-communist variety of capitalism. In this residual bloc, we also included the three Baltic countries (Estonia, Latvia, Lithuania) because these countries, despite the fact that they are part of the natural geographic region of North Europe (Figure 1), are – in our opinion – closer to the post-communist bloc, due to their history, culture, and economy, as also corroborated by their medium-low average levels of labour productivity (see Table 1).

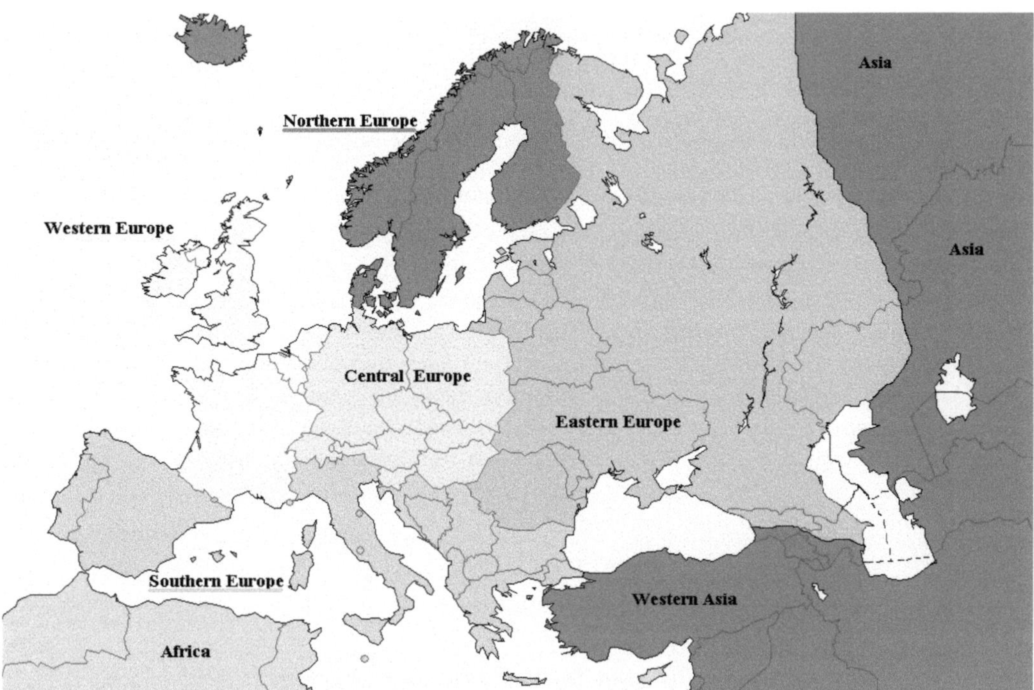

Source: United Nations Organization (UNO)

Figure 1: Classification of European countries by natural regions

1. The four big countries of Southern Europe being representative of the mixed (Mediterranean) model of capitalism: Italy, Spain, Portugal, and Greece. These countries encompass our main research object and show moderate levels of labour productivity.

2. The three countries of Western Europe following a liberal (Anglo-Saxon) model of capitalism: Ireland, the Netherlands, the U.K. These countries show a level of labour productivity higher than the average.

3. The three countries of Northern Europe following a social democratic (Scandinavian) model of capitalism: Denmark, Finland, and Sweden. These countries show a level of labour productivity higher than the average as well.

4. The four countries of western-central Europe following a corporatist (continental) model of capitalism: Austria, Belgium, France, and Germany. These countries show higher levels of labour productivity.

For building these blocs we took into account the diverse geographical areas of Europe according to the natural regions classification by the United Nations Organization (UNO; Figure 1), together with the scheme provided by the varieties of capitalism literature, according to Hall, Soskice (2001) and the extension realized by Amable (2003).[4]

We searched the content of available international surveys on issues like work and social values in order to identify measures for comparing many national varieties of work organization that exist across countries. We selected relevant and updated indicators relating to the EU-28 countries. Finally, we decided to analyse a set of indicators from the 5th and 6th waves of the EWCS (EUROFOUND 2016) as independent variables. Specifically, for each country, we used the percentage of surveyed workers affirming that:

1. Work less than 30/34 hours each week ('underloaded workers')

2. Work more than 40 hours each week ('overloaded workers')

---

[4]However, Amable (2003, p. 14) pointed out clearly that the geographical correspondence of some models of capitalism in Europe should not be taken too literally, but only for "the sake of simplicity".

3. Have rigid schedules to enter/exit at work ('rigid entry/exit schedule')

4. Work approximately the same number of hours every day ('rigid workday schedule')

The first two indicators refer to the amount of time employed for working, identifying the size of two groups of workers: on the one hand, underloaded workers, working a small number of hours each week (less than 30 in the 2010 survey, and less than 34 in the 2015 survey); on the other hand, overloaded workers, working more than 40 hours each week. Similarly, these data are compared with the real number of hours worked per week as reported by Eurostat for the year 2015. The latter two variables refer to the flexibility of working time, reflecting the rigidity of the national organizational model.

In summary, we analyse the relation between each one of these independent variables with the aggregated productivity at national level for each hour worked (dependent variable) as reported by Eurostat in 2010 and 2014 (data for 2015 are not available at the time of writing this paper). For each pair of variables (one by each wave), we built a scatter plot and estimated the lineal or polynomic slope and the correspondent coefficient of determination. The statistical formula behind this method is the following:

$$Y_{it} = \beta_1 X_{jit}^2 + \beta_0 X_{jit} + K \tag{1}$$

Where:

$Y_{it} \ldots$ Productivity per worked hour for the country i of year t

$X_{jit} \ldots$ Independent variable ('j' being the proportion of 'underloaded workers', 'overloaded workers', or 'workers with rigid entry/exit schedule' or 'rigid workday schedule' respectively) for the country i of year t

$K \ldots$ constant (intercept) of the model

The model has been estimated following a regular least squares regression procedure, performed through the Excel software.

In this way, we try to highlight the diverse outcomes obtained by geographic area, relating indicators of the number of hours worked and the flexibility of work schedules with labour productivity performance.

4 Findings

In this section, we describe the main findings of the study. We first tackle the trends underlying the data on labour productivity per worked hour (the dependent variable). This is followed by the results of the analyses of how productivity is influenced by the selected independent variables.

4.1 Productivity per Worked Hour Within EU-28

Table 1 shows the data on the levels of labour productivity of the 28 countries of the EU. We selected this measure for productivity due to the relation between GDP and the total number of hours that have been worked within the country. In this case, values have been standardized according to the average for the EU-28, which is 100 for each year. Countries have been ranked from higher levels to lower levels of productivity, taking 2010 as the reference year.

Looking at Table 1, we observe a few significant variations in the levels of labour productivity of countries between 2010 and 2014. Following the classification of natural regions, countries showing a higher than average levels of productivity are part of the Western Area (Luxembourg, Belgium, The Netherlands, Ireland, France) with the exception of the U.K., followed by Northern countries (Denmark, Sweden, Finland) and two countries of central Europe (Germany, Austria). Southern European countries occupy positions ranging from the EU-28 average (Italy, Spain) to lower than average levels (Greece, Portugal), along with the U.K., the Mediterranean countries and islands (Cyprus, Malta) and some countries of central Europe (Slovenia, Slovakia, Czech Republic). Eastern countries occupy the lower positions of the EU-28 labour productivity ranking.

Table 1: Comparing productivity between European countries

Country	2010	2014
LU – Luxembourg	173.9	182.0
BE – Belgium	138.4	134.7
NL – Netherlands	132.2	129.5
IE – Ireland	128.9	129.0
FR – France	128.8	128.0
DK – Denmark	129.9	127.1
DE – Germany	126.1	127.0
SE – Sweden	118.1	114.8
AT – Austria	113.5	113.4
FI – Finland	110.0	106.5
IT – Italy	103.7	101.7
ES – Spain	99.5	101.1
EU28 - European Union (28 countries)	*100.0*	*100.0*
UK - United Kingdom	104.8	99.7
CY – Cyprus	86.8	81.9
SI – Slovenia	77.6	79.3
SK – Slovakia	74.8	76.8
MT – Malta	75.9	71.4
CZ - Czech Republic	69.1	70.7
GR – Greece	75.2	70.6
PT – Portugal	68.6	70.1
HU – Hungary	67.3	65.6
LT – Lithuania	58.7	64.8
EE – Estonia	60.7	62.9
HR – Croatia	56.4	60.5
PL – Poland	55.9	58.6
LV – Latvia	49.6	53.6
RO – Romania	43.7	49.4
BG – Bulgaria	41.7	42.5

Source: EUROSTAT

By contrast, if we follow the classification of European countries according to the varieties of capitalism scheme, we observe that countries from two groups occupy the higher productivity positions: the corporatist bloc (Belgium, Germany, France, and Austria) and the liberal bloc, excepting the U.K. (The Netherlands and Ireland). These are closely followed by the social-democratic bloc of countries (Table 1). Next we find the bigger countries of the mixed bloc (Italy, Spain) along with some countries of the Anglo-Saxon area. Finally, we find the other two 'mixed' economies down the ranking, together with the post-communist economies.

In summary, differences in the level of labour productivity correspond to both geographical patterns and models of capitalism. Specifically, we may identify a strong cluster of countries in north-western Europe formed by a combination of countries following either a liberal or corporatist model, encompassing a kind of 'productive European heart'. While the Scandinavian countries show similar levels of productivity, the Mediterranean countries recorded lower levels of productivity.

4.2 Labour Productivity and Number of Worked Hours

The analysis of the national behaviour relating to labour productivity implies looking at the differences in terms of time dedicated to the workday. We show the existing relationship between the aggregate levels of productivity per worked hour of each country (the dependent variable) and the percentage of underloaded workers in 2010 (Figure 2) and 2015 (Figure 3). We observe that Southern European countries show a percentage of

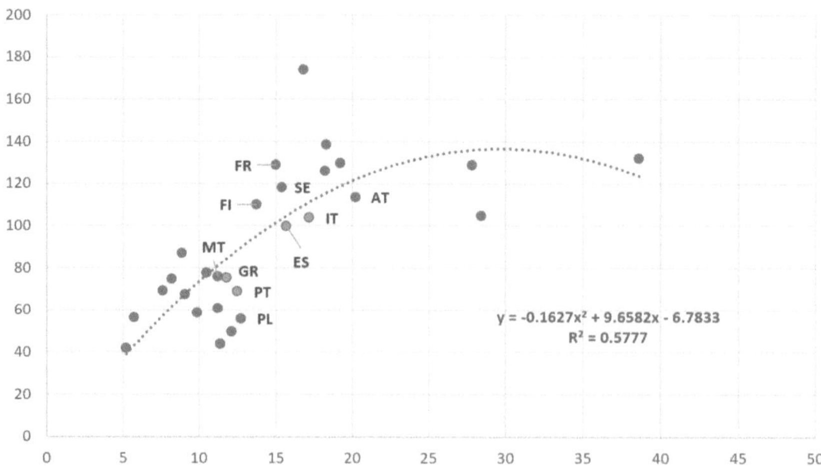

Source: EWCS

Figure 2: relation between productivity (y-axis) and percent of underloaded workers (x-axis) 2010

underloaded workers close to the average: between 11% and 18% for 2010, and between 18% and 27% for 2015, excepting in the case of Italy for this year (something more than 30% of its workforce).

Both in 2010 (Figure 2) and 2015 (Figure 3), we observe that there is a significant correlation between labour productivity and the percentage of underloaded workers, as exemplified by the (adjusted) coefficient of determination, higher than 0.5 in both cases. The relation between both variables is illustrated by a positive 2nd grade polynomic slope, growing faster in correspondence with lower levels of the independent variable (underloaded workers), and starting to decrease around a threshold of 30% for 2010 and 45% for 2015 (the difference is probably due to the diverse way of operationalizing the variable). This means that increasing the percentage of underloaded workers has a positive effect on productivity, at least until a certain threshold. In fact, all countries exceeding the European average (100) show a percentage of underloaded workers greater than the average (13% for 2010, 18% for 2015).

Graphs 3 and 4 show the relation between the levels of aggregated productivity per worked hour and the percentages of overloaded workers for each country. Most of Southern European countries show relatively elevated levels for this indicator (between 21% and 25%) while Greece leads the ranking both years with more than 43% of overloaded workers on its total workforce.

Both in 2010 and 2015 we observe a moderate correlation between productivity and overloaded workers, exemplified by the (adjusted) coefficient of determination, higher than 0.34 for 2010, and higher than 0.43 for 2015. The relation between these two variables is adequately illustrated by a negative 2nd grade polynomic slope, decreasing faster in correspondence with lower levels of the independent variable (overloaded workers) and starting to increase at a threshold of around 35% of the distribution. This means that increasing the percentage of overloaded workers has a negative effect on productivity, at least until a certain threshold. In fact, all countries exceeding the European average (100) show a percentage of overloaded workers lower than the average (around 25-27%).

What do these findings mean for understanding labour productivity in Southern Europe? The most relevant implication is that productivity per hour worked does not seem to increase depending only on the mere number of working hours. In other words, most productive countries are those in which there is a significant percentage of underloaded workers (more than a third of the total workforce) and a low percentage of overloaded workers (less than a quarter of the total workforce). Furthermore, workers of Mediterranean countries spend more time working than their counterparts in Liberal, Corporatist, and Social-Democratic countries. The Southern bloc countries struggle to increase their levels of productivity, given their higher level of extra hours (Table 1).

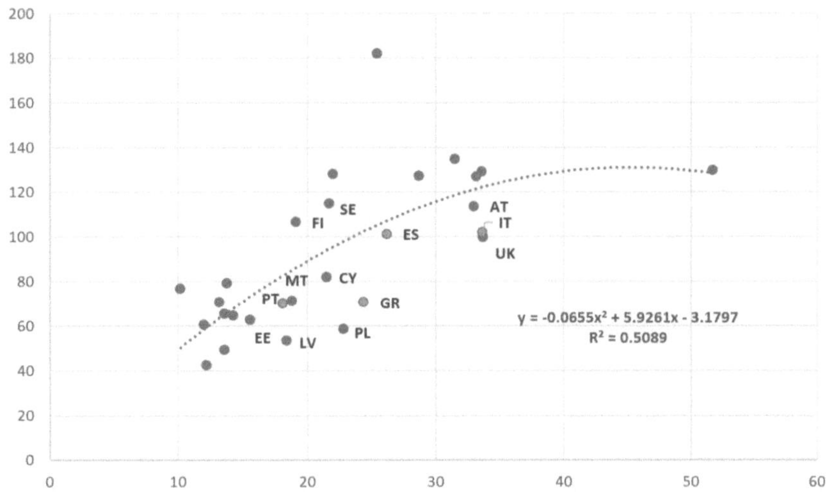

Source: EWCS

Figure 3: relation between productivity (*y*-axis) and percent of underloaded workers (*x*-axis), 2015

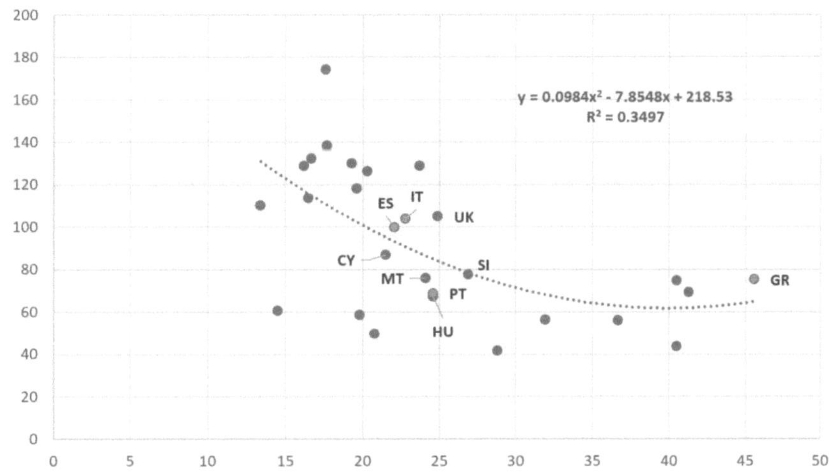

Source: EWCS

Figure 4: Relation between productivity (*y*-axis) and overloaded workers (*x*-axis), 2010

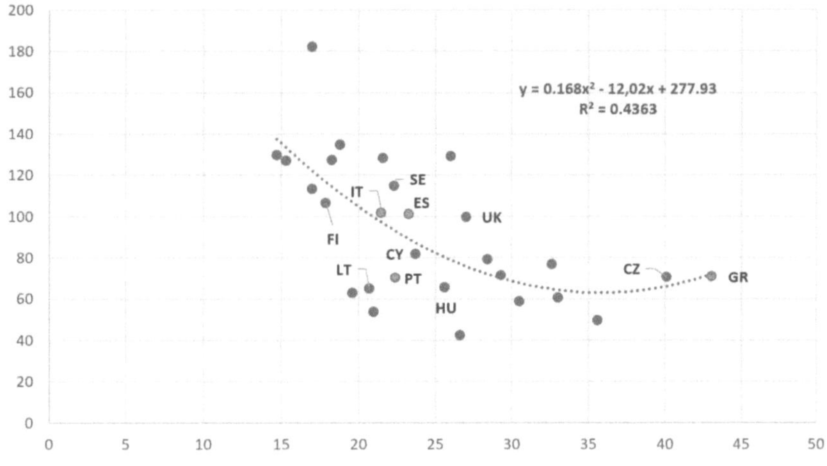

Source: EWCS

Figure 5: Relation between productivity (*y*-axis) and overloaded workers (*x*-axis), 2015

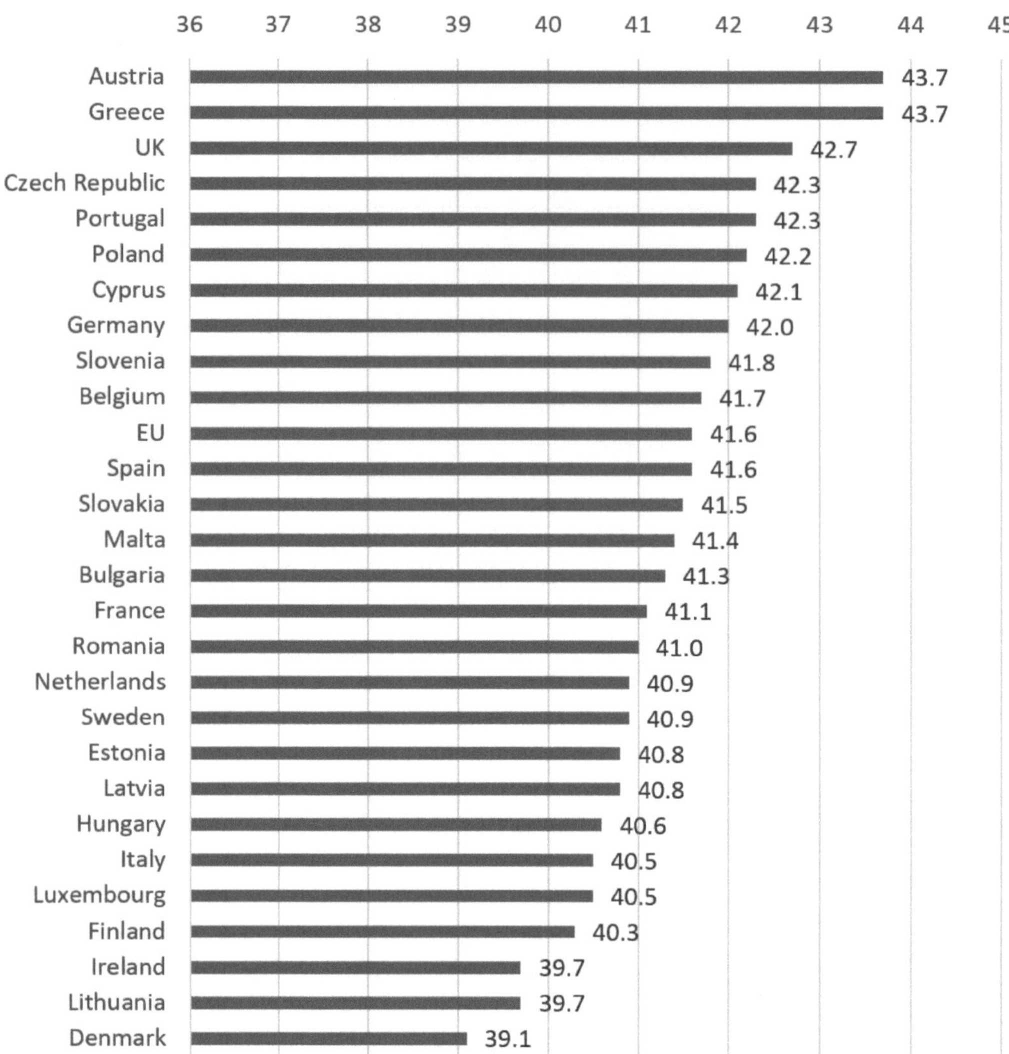

Source: EUROSTAT

Figure 6: Average of real worked hours by European countries, 2012

Another illustration of the amount of time spent working in the countries is included in the Eurostat data relating to the average of real worked hours by European countries in 2012 (Figure 6). Excluding the opposite cases of Austria (higher levels of both productivity and worked hours) and Lithuania (lower levels of both), this distribution corroborates our findings. The less productive countries of the Mediterranean area (Portugal and Greece) appear within the top five countries that dedicate most time to work. While Spain occupies a position close to the EU average, Italy exhibits medium-low levels of working hours. In turn, we find four of the most productive countries of the continent (Luxembourg, Ireland, Denmark, and Finland) among the five countries that dedicate less time to work.

Furthermore, the difference in terms of economic performance between Mediterranean countries and the other three blocs is influenced by a higher number of hours dedicated to work. In reality, it seems that a reduction of working time is a kind of 'recompense' for achieving certain levels of productivity. This virtuous relation seems particularly evident in Scandinavian countries. By contrast, we can imagine that the limited productivity of Southern countries implies an extension of their workdays. Such circumstances suggest we focus our attention on the cultural and organizational factors that inhibit productivity. Specifically, we analyse how productivity is influenced by factors such as the flexibility or the rigidness of working schedule.

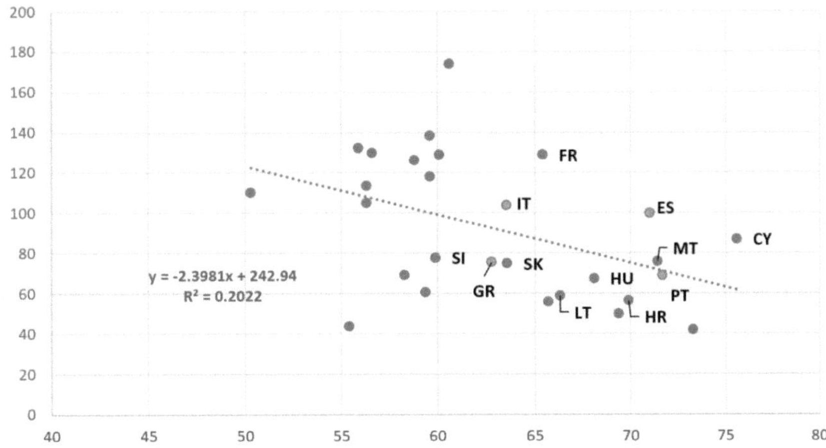

Source: EWCS

Figure 7: Relation between productivity (*y*-axis) and rigid entry/exit schedule (*x*-axis), 2010

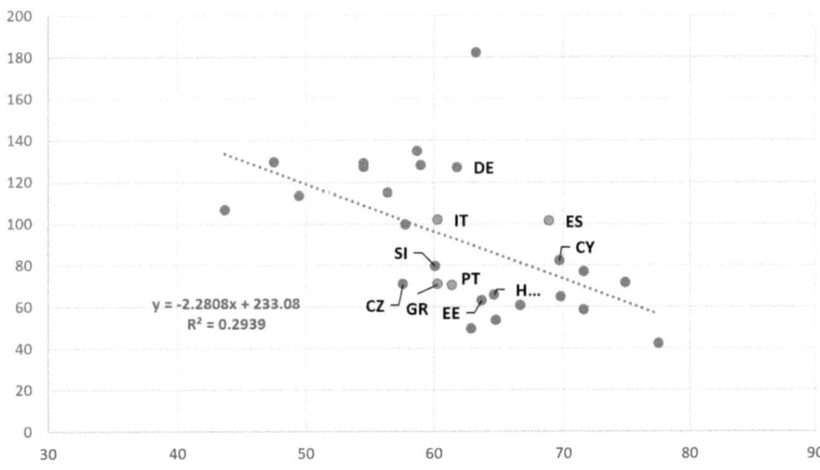

Source: EWCS

Figure 8: Relation between productivity (*y*-axis) and rigid entry/exit schedule (*x*-axis), 2015

4.3 Labour Productivity and Flexible Organizational Models

Figure 7 (2010) and Figure 8 (2015) show the relation between the aggregate levels of productivity per worked hour for each country, and the percentage of workers with a rigid entry/exit schedule. In both years, Mediterranean countries show a clear rigidity of entry and exit times at work when compared with the rest of Europe exhibiting values higher than 60% with even higher percentages for Portugal and Spain (more than 72% of their total workforces in 2010).

We observe a moderate correlation between labour productivity and the percentage of workers with a rigid entry/exit schedule. The relation between the two variables is exemplified by a negative linear slope. A coefficient of determination of 0.20 is estimated for 2010 (Figure 7) and 0.29 for 2015 (Figure 8). This means that those countries with high percentages of workers on a rigid entry-exit schedule exhibit lower levels of labour productivity. Specifically, we observe that all countries with productivity levels higher than the European average (100) exhibit a more flexible organizational model in terms of entry/exit times at work: their percentages are lower than 60%, excluding France in 2010, and Luxembourg and Germany in 2015.

Figure 9 (2010) and Figure 10 (2015) show the relation between the aggregate levels

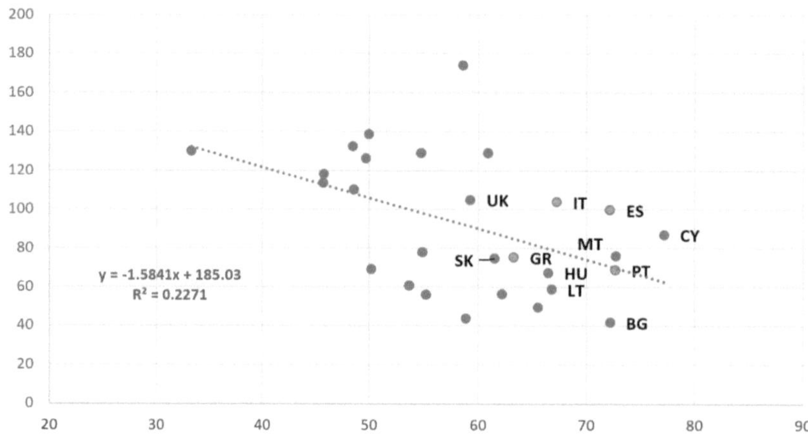

Source: EWCS

Figure 9: Relation between productivity (y-axis) and rigid workday schedule (x-axis), 2010

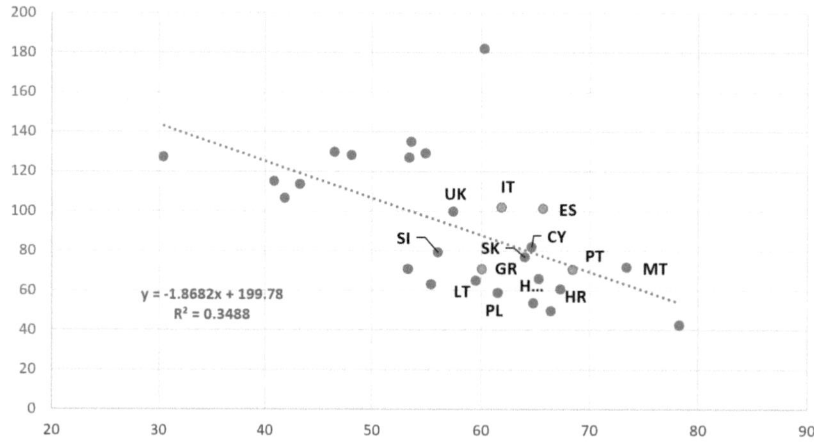

Source: EWCS

Figure 10: Relation between productivity (y-axis) and rigid workday schedule (x-axis), 2015

of productivity per worked hour for each country, and the percentage of workers with a rigid workday schedule. It is clear that Mediterranean countries exhibit a higher level of workers with rigid workday schedules: more than 60% in all cases and more than two thirds of the total workforce of Spain and Portugal.

We observe a moderate correlation between labour productivity and the percentage of workers with a rigid workday schedule. The relation between the two variables is exemplified by a negative linear slope. A coefficient of determination of 0.23 is estimated for 2010 (Figure 9) and 0.35 for 2015 (Figure 10). This means that countries with rigid workday schedules exhibit lower levels of labour productivity. This is the case with Mediterranean countries, exhibiting values higher than 60% both in 2010 and 2015. By contrast, we observe that all those countries with levels of productivity higher than the European average (100) exhibit more flexible organizational models in terms of daily distribution of working hours: their values are all lower than 60% in all cases.

Furthermore, our findings show that the most productive European countries exhibit organizational traits oriented toward shorter workdays and stronger flexibility of schedules. By contrast, Mediterranean countries (Italy, Spain, Portugal, Greece) have longer workdays (less in the case of Italy) and a more rigid organizational model of work time management. The divide between the Mediterranean area and the other three 'leading' varieties of capitalism is clear.

5 Conclusions

We affirm the existence of relevant differences in terms of labour productivity levels between European countries according to geographical areas and national models of work time management. Following the classification schemes proposed by UNO and the varieties of capitalism literature (Hall, Soskice 2001, Amable 2003), we identified the existence of relevant differences in Europe between Western-Central countries (corporatist model), North-Western (liberal), Northern (social democratic), and the South (mixed-Mediterranean). The level of productivity per worked hour is higher in the first three blocs or more specifically, in the European productive heart. In contrast, Mediterranean countries exhibit intermediate (Spain, Italy) or lower (Greece, Portugal) levels of productivity per worked hour.

Furthermore, we observed that those countries with higher levels of productivity also exhibit lower levels of average real worked hours with the Mediterranean countries clearly positioned above the EU average (partial exception: Italy). While Mediterranean workers spend more time at work, their productivity levels are lower. This suggests the existence of a different work performance during the workday that is probably due to its longer extension and the influence of private-family issues on labour dynamics. Phenomena that are likely to have evolved from historical, cultural, and institutional issues such as the high diffusion of split-by-half workdays and the tradition of moonlighting. The resulting organizational disorder that creates 'eternal' workdays (Simmel 1998, Paugam 2007) is likely to create the impression that Mediterranean countries enter into a cycle of 'overloading' to compensate for the waste of less productive work time when confronted with the pressures of global competition and economic recession. A phenomenon that places a very high responsibility on families (and, especially, on adult women) in terms of social welfare as outlined in the Mediterranean organizational model of family care (Pfirsch 2013). In this sense, the forms of governance of the Mediterranean countries, with manifestations close to "neopatrimonialism", have reduced the potential for development of the Welfare State and, therefore, for properly developing their organization of work (Bechle 2010).

The economic performance of the most productive European countries depends on a set of cultural, organizational, and technological factors that foster labour productivity. Among these factors is the development of a flexible organizational model for work time management based on flexible entry/exit times at work and a flexible number of working hours per day. In contrast, the Mediterranean countries have evolved differently by adopting a rigid organizational model for both entry/exit times at work and the number of working hours per day, with negative consequences for productivity.

We conclude this study with a call for positive change. Looking at the recent decline of the European economy, we observe that the recent efforts of EU policies (and its powerful array of public aids) to reduce north-south imbalances have not achieved the expected results (González Rodríguez et al. 2000, De la Fuente 2005). This comparative (even if superficial) analysis of the Southern European economies contributes to a deeper appreciation of some significant factors underlying the recent episode of 'European decadence' within the global system of politico-economic relations. When evaluating future policy initiatives to rebalance the Mediterranean economies, we recommend that consideration should not only be given to the impact on productivity, but also be given to the roles to be played by national institutions in shaping the organizational models for managing work time and other labour issues. Among the various options open to national institutions, we highlight work time flexibility as an organizational strategy and value. As structural and cultural barriers such as the weight of bureaucracy and traditions are overtaken, fostering such flexibility can contribute to an increase in labour productivity in Southern European countries. Furthermore, there are worthwhile incentives to foster an institutional and organizational change in labour practices to adopt flexible work time management strategies including increased workers' satisfaction, greater work-family conciliation and reduced costs due to less work overloading.

References

Amable B (2003) *The diversity of modern capitalism.* Oxford University Press, Oxford, UK. CrossRef.

Amable B (2009) Structural reforms in Europe and the (in)coherence of institutions. *Oxford Review of Economic Policy* 25[1]: 17–39. CrossRef.

Baldwin JR, Brown WM, Maynard JP (2005) Interprovincial differences in GDP per capita, labour productivity and work intensity: 1990-2003. No. 2005011e, Statistics Canada, Economic Analysis

Banfield E (1958) *The moral basics of a backward society.* The Free Press, Glencoe, IL

Basque Governement (2010) Estudio sobre las implicaciones y posibles consecuencias de un cambio horario laboral en el tejido empresarial de la CAPV, de cara a conseguir una mayor conciliación de la vida laboral and familiar. Gobierno Vasco, Departamento de Empleo and Asuntos Sociales. Vitoria

Bechle K (2010) Neopatrimonialism in Latin America: Prospects and promises of a neglected concept. Legitimacy and efficiency of political systems (GICA Research Program). Nr 153

Bratton M, Van de Walle N (1997) *Democratic experiences in Africa. Regime transitions in comparative perspective.* Cambridge University Press, Cambridge, UK

Brennetot A, Emsellem K, Guérin-Pace F, Garnier B (2013) Dire l'Europe à travers le monde. *Cybergeo: European Journal of Geography 630.* CrossRef.

Cassano F (1996) *Il pensiero meridiano.* Laterza, Roma-Bari

Castells M (1997) *La era de la información.* Alianza, Madrid

Crouch C (1998) Esiste una società europea? *Stato e mercato* 2: 167–202

De Jong HW (1995) European capitalism: Between freedom and social justice. *Review of Industrial Organization* 10[4]: 399–419. CrossRef.

De la Fuente A (2005) El impacto de la reducción de las ayudas estructurales europeas: Una primera aproximación. *Presupuesto y gasto público* 39: 173–190

Esping-Andersen G (1999) *Los tres mundos del Estado del bienestar.* Alfons el Magnánim, Valencia

EUROFOUND (2016) European working conditions survey. Acceded in 6th of July 2016, on the web site of: EUROFOUND: http://www.eurofound.europa.eu

Feld L, Otero M, Weigert B (2015) Putting Germany's 'minijobs' in their context. El País (15/10/2015). Available at https://elpais.com/elpais/2015/10/15/inenglish/-1444918067_940829.html

González Rodríguez M, Martín Poveda E, Martínez García S, Santamaría Fidalgo J (2000) La desigualdad Norte-Sur en la Unión Europea. Universidad Complutense de Madrid: VII Jornadas de Economía Crítica

Guillén M (1994) *Models of management: work, authority, and organization in a comparative perspective.* University of Chicago Press, Chicago, IL

Halbwachs M (2002) Les causes de suicide. Coll. Le Lien Social. Paris, originally published 1930. CrossRef.

Hall PA, Soskice D (2001) *Varieties of capitalism: The institutional foundations of comparative advantage.* Oxford University Press, Oxford, UK. CrossRef.

Hall RE, Jones CI (1996) The productivity of nations. No. w5812, National Bureau of Economic Research. CrossRef.

Hill J, Grzywacz S, Allen V, Blanchard V, Matz-Costa C, Shulkin S, Pitt-Catsouphes M (2008) Defining and conceptualizating work place flexibility. *Community Work and Family* 11: 149–163. CrossRef.

Inglehart R (1997) *Modernization and Postmodernization.* Princeton University Press, Princeton, NJ. CrossRef.

Jijena-Michel D, Jijena-Michel C (2015) El rol moderador de la flexibilidad del horario de trabajo en la relación del enriquecimiento trabajo familia y la satisfacción docente. *Horizontes Empresariales* 10[2]: 41–56

Lambert S (2000) Added benefits the link between work-life benefits and organizational citizenship behaviour. *Academy of Management Journal* 43: 801–815. CrossRef.

Lamo de Espinosa E (2010) *Europa después de Europa.* Academia Europa de las Ciencias and las Artes, Madrid

Leonardi L, Martín A, Molina O, Calenda D, Carrasquer P (2011) ¿Es exportable la flexiseguridad? Un estudio comparado de Italia y España. *Cuadernos de Relaciones Laborales* 29[2]: 417–443. CrossRef.

Lewis S (2003) Flexible working arrangements: Implementations, outcomes and management. In: Cooper C, Roberts I (eds), *Annual Review of Industrial Psychology,* Volume 18. Wiley-Blackwell, New York, NY, 1–28. CrossRef.

López-Pintor R, Wert J (1982) La otra España: Insolidaridad e intolerancia en la tradición político-cultural española. *Revista Española de Investigaciones Sociológicas* 19: 292–307

Lusa A, et al (2007) Gestión de los horarios de trabajo en presencia de cláusulas de flexibilidad pasiva. *Universia Business Review* 14[2]: 10–25

Maya M (2016) *El ocaso del chavismo. Venezuela (2005-2015).* Alfa, Montevideo, Uruguay

Maynard JP (2007) The comparative level of GDP per capita in Canada and the United States: A decomposition into labour productivity and work intensity differences. The Canadian Productivity Review, 15-206

Meardi G (2012) Mediterranean capitalism'under EU pressure: Labour market reforms in Spain and Italy, 2010-2012. *Warsaw Forum of Economic Sociology* 3[1]: 51–81

MGI – McKinsey Global Institute (2010) Más allá de la austeridad: Un camino hacia el crecimiento económico y la renovación en Europa. McKinsey Global Institute. London, UK. Available at http://www.mckinsey.com/insights/mgi/research/productivity_competitiveness

Migdal J (1998) *Strong societies and weak states: State-society relations and state capabilities in the Third World.* Princeton University Press, Princeton NJ

Miguélez F, Prieto C (2009) Transformaciones del empleo, flexibilidad y relaciones laborales en Europa. *Política and Sociedad* 46[2]: 275–287

Moerland PW (1995) Corporate ownership and control structures: An international comparison. *Review of industrial organization* 110[4]: 443–464. CrossRef.

Paugam S (2007) *Las formas elementales de la pobreza.* Alianza, Madrid

Perrons D (2005) Gender mainstreaming and gender equality in the new economy. An analysis of contradiction. *International Journal of Politics* 7[4]: 389–411

Pfirsch T (2013) Une géographie de la famille en Europe du Sud. *Cybergeo: European Journal of Geography. 533.* CrossRef.

Pizzorno A (1966) Amoral familism and historical marginality. *International Review of Community Development* 15: 55–66

Regini M (1995) La varietà italiana di capitalismo. Istituzioni sociali e struttura produttiva negli anni Ottanta. *Stato e mercato* 43[2]: 3–21

Segura J (2006) *La productividad en la economía española.* Fundación Ramón Areces, Madrid

Simmel G (1998) Les pauvres. Coll. Cuadrige, Paris. Originally published 1907

Van de Walle N (2005) Economic reform. Patterns of constraints. In: Gyimah-Boahdi E (ed), *Democratic reform in Africa. The quality of progress.* Lynne Rienner, Boulder, CO

Villena A (2017) *¿Cómo se gobierna España? La estructura de las élites gubernamentales en 2004 y 2016.* Comares, Granada, Spain

The Journal of ERSA
Powered by WU

Volume 6, Number 1, 2019, 25–44
DOI: 10.18335/region.v6i1.207

journal homepage: region.ersa.org

Similitudes and singularities of higher education systems in the Mediterranean countries: Historical construction, policy and evolution of key indicators

Cláudia Urbano[1]

[1] Universidada Nova de Lisboa, Lisbon, Portugal

Received: 14 September 2017/Accepted: 10 July 2019

Abstract. Higher education is one of the most important areas for societies moving towards development and modernity. Analysing higher education systems in Europe, it is clear that Southern Europe has many differences from the rest of the continent, despite the strategies to achieve a European higher education culture by implementing reforms on all European countries' higher education systems on the basis of common key values. Taking into account four Southern Europe countries – Portugal, Spain, Italy and Greece – and regarding their link to a certain Mediterranean culture, the proposal is to analyse these four countries' higher education systems and their growth, using indicators for educational and economic development. This paper provides a reflection on a hypothetically similar evolutionary pattern according to a hypothetically similar historical cultural background, as well as on a set of external stimuli provided by modernization and Europeanization processes. The relation between higher education and the labour market will be analysed, understanding it as a relevant 'third mission' policy for higher education systems. By identifying these countries' educational, cultural and socioeconomic similitudes and singularities, the reflection aims to reinforce and enrich a sociological analysis of the existence of a Southern European approach to higher education as a specific value in Mediterranean culture. To better understand large transformation processes, a comparative analysis on the institutional and policy making levels will be used. At the same time, suggesting how modernization theory informed the evolution of higher education systems in the four countries through higher education policy and contributing to regional strategies for development.

1 Introduction

From a sociological point of view, there are three possible ways to approach the theme of higher education: 1) based on sociology of education, the focus could be on the actions of higher education students and its relation to social reproduction; 2) based on pedagogy, the focus could be higher education learning processes and pedagogical models; or 3) based on public policy, the focus could be the definition of a higher education public policy and how it is perceived by social actors and how it is transposed to results. Despite considering the importance of all of the three perspectives, the exercise proposed is to provide a reflection about the third way, focusing on higher education and its relation to society and economy.

Higher education is one of the most important key values in modern societies. It generates broader economic growth as well as individual success. In 1998, The World Declaration on Higher Education (UNESCO 1998) underlined the preservation, reinforcement and further expansion of education, training, and research as core missions of higher education systems. Additional foci included contributing to the sustainable development and improvement of society as a whole. Further, "higher education has acquired an unprecedented role in present-day society, as a vital component of cultural, social, economic and political development" (UNESCO 1998, p. 1).

Higher education systems first mission is nation- and state building and of supplying educated manpower, "designed to shape the national elite, the senior officials and graduates in the public sector services" (Stamelos, Paivandi 2015, p. 2). Its second mission is academic training and scientific knowledge. A third mission was added to higher education systems: regional development and community engagement, supplying knowledge-intense outputs, and a fundamental contribution to economic growth and regional development (Paleari et al. 2014). As these authors state, in the transition from pre-modern to modern societies in Europe, changes in higher education emerged to respond to the changing demands and needs of the society and stakeholders.

Higher education systems' social function is to qualify people to work as specialists, professionals and highly qualified human resource to meet the needs of governments, industry, business and all branches of society. Besides training, higher education systems also provide a range of services and research outputs to the community and it has a role in the national and institutional policy-making and economic, technological, social and cultural reforms. Pure knowledge is no longer and not only what society expects from a higher education system. It is also supposed to fulfil social, scientific, economic and technological needs as well as respond to demands from society. Public policies towards higher education are directly and indirectly defined to achieve goals other than just purely knowledge.

There is a growing recognition of the potential role of higher education institutions as a driver of national and regional economic development (Newlands 2003). As stated by the renewed EU Agenda for Higher Education adopted by the European Commission in 2017 (European Comission 2017, 247 final), higher education is an important asset for regional development and competitiveness. It can boost innovation and upgrade the skills of the workforce through education and lifelong learning. First at a regional level, then at a national and finally at the European level. Linking higher education to the labour market is thinking of development in a broader perspective than just economic prosperity (Angelis et al. 2016). It is the incorporation of a social dimension, carried out in every country and specifically in every region. As Newlands states, "universities add to the human capital of the region and assist the innovative processes of firms but in turn their teaching and research activities are informed by businesses in the region" (Newlands 2003, p. 1).

A practical, useful, applied but at the same time highly qualified knowledge is an indispensable engine of the society. As Paleari et al write, "historically the development of higher education is closely related to the growth of economy and society and university's mission evolved during the centuries to respond to the changing societal needs" (Paleari et al. 2014, p. 369). Social and economic evidence of the outcomes of higher education is measured in terms of the growth of the economy and society. Higher education is a 'cultural reference point' for each society, besides having an essential role as a social institution and a provider and supporter of the society's innovation system (Paleari et al. 2014).

In a globalised world, countries share guidelines on higher education and import from each other's best practices (Kivinen, Nurmi 2003). Besides, some countries' education systems are already quite similar based on historical, geographical or cultural aspects.

The focus of this paper on higher education systems in some European Mediterranean countries is justified by the fact that Southern Europe has been determining many differences from the rest of the continent, despite the effort of the Bologna Process to ensure comparability in the standards and quality of higher education qualifications. Taking four Southern Europe and Mediterranean countries sharing a historical political cultural and social identity (Sprague 2016) – Portugal, Spain, Italy and Greece – as the object of analysis, the proposal of this paper is to discuss in which way there is a shared experience of higher education in order to sustain the concept of a Mediterranean culture toward higher education. This will be based on some similitude in cultural historical social political economic and educational characteristics. The relation between higher education and the labour market are the dimensions of the analysis.

First, similitudes and singularities of the four countries regarding higher education will be discussed. Its characterization, the important social and political changes in the last decades in each of these Mediterranean countries and the countries' public policies on higher education as a consequence, will sustain this first structural comparison.

Considering the social function of a higher education system as responding to the needs of society and stakeholders, the second stage of the reflection is to evaluate the relation between higher education and the qualification of the labour market in the four countries. Using international data sources, such as OECD and Eurostats, based on reliable, official and governmental data to explore statistical trends, this empirical reflection will help to compare the four countries' higher education culture(s) between them and the European Union average. This will allow for understanding how far the social construction of the concept of a Mediterranean higher education culture is sustainable.

Finally, after the analysis of the data, some emergent questions will be pointed out in order to enrich the debate surrounding a Mediterranean higher education culture.

This analysis can provide important clues not only to the definition of national strategies and policy on higher education and a high-skill labour market, but also for regional developments, investments in higher education and local industries.

2 Background

2.1 The missions of a higher education System

Similar to other dimensions of society, education in general and higher education in particular have certain roles and missions in societies. Considering higher education, instead of being replaced by another, different missions and goals have been added to the initial one. The first mission – education – was mainly focused on nation- and state building as well as increasing society's educated manpower. 'Scientification' was a second mission of higher education systems, through defining academic training and scientific knowledge. In both missions, pure knowledge was the common ground. A third mission was added to higher education when knowledge needed to be operationalized as a fundamental role for economic growth and regional development (Paleari et al. 2014). As Antonowicz (2012), the human capital theory, as the theoretical framework most responsible for the adoption of education and development policies, rests on the assumption that formal education is highly instrumental and even necessary to improve the population's production capacity.

Since their beginning, universities are par excellence the institutions of production of knowledge. But knowledge is not locked inside the institutions and has been transferred and used in societies towards development and modernization. In present day knowledge economies and societies, higher education institutions have become politically and economically more important as institutions that produce and transfer knowledge. As Krings states, "we are living in knowledge-based societies; we are knowledge-based workers; we are working in knowledge-intensive sectors and we are producing knowledge-intensive services" (Krings 2006, p. 9). Or, as in Drucker's model (Drucker 1969, cited by Antonowicz (2012)), the production of goods is being gradually replaced by the provision of services, and knowledge and skills are playing an increasing role in the national economy.

That is why it is no longer possible to think of higher education without considering its relation to the labour market as a specific dimension of modern societies and economies. But firstly, a reflection on the historical, social, cultural and political context surrounding the development of higher education systems must be provided.

2.2 Conceptualizing a Mediterranean higher education culture

Clustering countries according to specific parameters besides geographic ones is a way to structure an analysis striking a balance between generalization and specificity. The clustering process might take into account, separately or not, different dimensions: geographical, economic, political, social, demographical, to mention few. Criteria of comparison must be defined, and by doing so, some countries might not be included, in an objective but selective way, as encapsulating an entire region is not the researcher's aim.

Southern Europe can be regarded as a distinct regional entity, by its common climatic system and a geographical expression of strategic importance different from Northern Europe. Inside the European Mediterranean zone, different societies and economies have been developed. Similarities and shared experiences allow the grouping of Greece, Italy, Portugal and Spain together (Lazaridis 1996). Through sharing a certain common identity (Williams 1984), they can be grouped as a 'family of nations' with similar pattern of public policies.

The relevant literature on higher education systems leads to a first and considerable obstacle for the comparison: higher education in Europe, as well as globally, is very diverse. And labelling a country's higher education system as if it is homogeneous is to suggest a singular model of higher education discharging any possibility of inner diversity and, therefore, the model having a strong bias towards reality.

One of the first key studies of diversity in higher education systems is done by Birnbaum (1983), identifying seven categories of diversity: a) a systemic diversity, referring to differences in institutional type, size and control found; b) a structural diversity, resulting from historical and legal foundations; c) a programmatic diversity, according to the degree level or degree area, mission and main programmes and services provided by institutions; d) a procedural diversity, differing ways of teaching, researching and/or providing services of the institutions; e) a reputational diversity, as long as there might be differences in institutions by their status and prestige; f) a constituential diversity, by including a variety of institutional constituents such as faculty, staff, trustees, and political and religious interest groups; and g) a value and climate diversity, regarding the social environment and culture.

In a more recent perspective, also Teichler (2007) highlighted higher education diversity, adding a horizontal and a vertical approach, and focusing the importance of institutional missions and profiles as a criterion for a distinction. van Vught et al. (2010) suggested that a greater variety in the environmental conditions (particularly governmental policy contexts), and a variety of norms and values in which a higher education system operates is reflected in an institutional diversity of higher education institutions. Besides, "diversity would also increase if Europe's higher education institutions were operating within diverse policy contexts that were supportive of a variety of missions and profiles" (van Vught et al. 2010, p. 12).

Every higher education system is generally associated to a certain social, economic and educational profile despite having internal differences. Considering each profile's specificity, how is the comparison made between countries? By controlling exactly in which terms it may or may not be compared in different systems, certain trends can be drawn and specific similitudes and singularities can be identified. Doing so, an objective parameter of comparison is defined specifying similitudes (Foucault 1983, Hook 2007) and singularities (Deleuze 1990) of each research object.

Taking each higher education system as unique, and considering social, political, economic, geographical and educational characteristics of Portugal, Spain, Greece and Italy, their similitude is sustained in a sociological perspective searching for shared experiences and strategies towards higher education. In this line of thought, the concept of Mediterranean higher education culture must be considered. Despite each country's singularity, culture – from a sociological perspective – is the ensemble of symbolic codes, shared experiences, attitudes, beliefs, norms, practices, symbols and values.

The thought of a 'higher education culture' took its first steps in the early work of Clark (1973) by providing an important, original well-spring for work on culture in higher education (Maassen 1996). The concept of a culture in higher education included very different topics: culture regarding students' social backgrounds and multiculturalism inside the institutions; culture as a sense of organization inside the institutions; culture as an institutional environment and its influence on students. But a higher education culture is also seen in a macro perspective as a support for public policies and the definition of strategies towards the development of the society and the economy.

As Lazaridis (1996, p. 6) stated, between these countries there is an "element of common identity in relation to key socio-economic, politic-economic and cultural aspects and changes which have transformed the whole region in the last decades". Among several characteristics, such as economic styles, political cultures and institutions, family structures, industrial organizations, welfare state, migration trends, religion, etc., it is clear that the educational and specifically the higher education system can also be an element of a shared Mediterranean culture.

Several dimensions and indicators reflect a country's or institution's higher education culture, but not all of them are taken into account in this study. This study will exclude dimensions related to quality or governance, internationalisation or research. Instead, this study will focus more on those linked to the missions of a higher education public policy and its relation to economy and labour market as a higher education output to society and economy.

Indicators such as global trends, system's expansion, and population with tertiary education, graduates employment and unemployment are some of those considered in this analysis as comparable and characteriser of a higher education culture. Also public policies and socio-economic and political context must be included in this approach. The next chapter provides a brief context to the development of each country's higher education system. Afterwards, some statistical indicators regarding higher education and the labour market will be analysed.

2.3   Higher education and the social and political context in four Mediterranean countries

Even considering possible differences between the countries, researchers are best suited to understand the development of each higher education systems in the last decades through knowing their social, political and economic situation. The modernization strategies countries have outlined to reposition themselves within the modern world system have been shaping their higher education systems under the framework of increasingly competitive knowledge societies.

For this analysis, four Southern Europe countries were selected: Portugal, Spain, Italy and Greece. Besides being geographically located in the southern part of Europe and sharing Mediterranean waters and a certain Mediterranean culture, recently these countries have undergone a similar process of becoming part of European Union and adjusted to European rules.

This group of Mediterranean countries share a historical, political, cultural, and social identity. The historical and political realities of these distinct countries necessarily influence their education systems – from their system development to reforms over time and their current priorities (Sprague 2016). Specifically considering higher education, the Bologna Declaration (a joint statement of thirty-one European Ministers of Education signed on 19th June 1999), regarding education, is an example of how these societies' policies were defined in order to respond to Europe's call to harmonise European higher education systems. The Bologna process was a voluntary, intergovernmental process based on the open method of coordination, which aims at the align of national policies in order to achieve specific goals (Asderaki 2009). Mitchell, Nielsen (2012) argue the policy ideas circulating globally are also linked to international political organizations (the EU, World Bank, IMF, UN, UNESCO and OECD), representing "a complex and ungovernable web of relationships that extends beyond the nation state" (Waters 1995, cited by Mitchell, Nielsen (2012)).

Another common aspect between the four countries refers to its position in a globalized world. Despite the scientific controversy of classification nowadays, these four countries as peripheral (e.g. Gambarotto, Solari 2014) or semi-peripherical (e.g. Roncevic 2001) according to Wallerstein's World-Systems Theory (Wallerstein 1979). In both perspectives, their non-centrality is never open to question. And this is obvious considering their recent economic history, their struggle against economic and social crisis and the two-speed Europe (Vanhercke et al. 2016, Piris 2012).

Katrougalos, Lazaridis (2003) showed how difficult it is to characterize these four countries as completely similar, regarding their social policy developments and a broader political economic and social environment. In some indicators, there may be some divergence between the four countries, but in general their trends and characteristics are very different from other European countries. Their similarities and some singularities in their historical, socio-economic and socio-political context, with regards to higher educations over the last decades, will be summarized next. Before that, a description of each country's process of building a higher education system will be given, in an arbitrary order.

There were two major changes in the twentieth century that helped Portugal catch up with the rest of Europe considering the socio-political and socioeconomic context and the changes in several dimensions including higher education. Firstly, the Revolution of 1975, which led to significant democratic reforms. Secondly, Portugal's admission to the European Common Market, which provided substantial financial aid and technological cooperation. Concerning education, one of the major public policies on education was the Education System Basic Law (LBSE 46/1986) and its changes and adaptations to Bologna's educational culture in 2005 (Law 49/2005). Consequently, a renewed educational system helped reduce the educational gap, lowered the socioeconomic gap of the population, and increased the economic and technological development of the country. Since then, education in Portugal is developing at an accelerated rate: illiteracy rates have fallen consistently in the last years from around twenty per cent in 1998 to seven per cent in 2017, of the general population. The enrolment has increased dramatically from six per cent in 1998 up to eighteen per cent in 2017. The country has been developing rapidly and education is accompanying this strong evolution. The higher education system in Portugal is organized in two subsystems: university education and non-university higher education (polytechnic education). Higher education is provided through public and private universities and non-university higher education institutions (both public and private).

In Spain too, there were also important political changes, resulting in a reform on education. Within a short period, only a year and a half, Spain and Portugal both ended a long dictatorial period and began a process of political transformation leading to democratic regimes. Both countries were incorporated into the European Economic Community in 1986. Additionally, in both countries, the political, social and economic changes had consequences for the status of higher education. Notwithstanding the differences in each process of higher education reform, both countries started from the same strategic premise – the premise of modernization – with profound implications for public education policies. Considering the legal framework, the most important reform regarding higher education came with the adoption of the University Reform Act of 1983, where universities became a public service, and private universities were validated as higher education providers. The Spanish higher education system consists of both university and non-university institutions, although it operates more as a unitary system made up of only university institutions (Santiago et al. 2009). The principal law for tertiary education, the Organic Law on Universities (LOU, Ley Orgánica de Universidades, Law 6/2001 on Universities, 21 December 2001, amended by the Organic Law 4/2007, 12 April 2007) concerns universities only. Non-university tertiary education, consisting of post-secondary higher vocational education and specialised tertiary education, is regulated by the Organic Law on Education (LOE, Ley Orgánica de Educación of 2006). In 2009 the Spanish government launched a policy initiative, Estrategia Universidad 2015, aiming to boost the competitiveness of Spanish universities. As in other countries, internationalization was one of the main goals of the strategy. But the focus of this paper will be on other goals than strategy.

On the growth within the educational system in Spain, literature refers to a dramatic increase since the 1960s and continued during the 1970s and the 1980s: from around 100.000 students in 1950 up to more than 1.5 million by the end of the 1980s (Villarroya et al. 2008). During the general restructuration of the education system in 1990, the enrolment of students in the universities has almost doubled in ten years, between 1983 and 1993 (Díaz 2010). Subirats (2001) stated that the changes in Spanish university in the last three decades are incomparable with any other historical moment: an increase in the infrastructures and enrolments, but also inside the organizations and in the nature of the university's mission.

Historically, during the second half of the 20th century, the Italian Republic was founded in 1946 and the Italian Constitution came into effect in 1948. Also, Italy was a founding member of the Inner Six (the six founding member states of the European Communities) in 1951. These were significant events, which marked a turning page in Italy's post-Fascist history as well as the civil, social and economic consequences of World War II. In such a turbulent and intense socioeconomic and socio-political context, there were multiple reforms in education in general and specifically higher education. Particularly during the past 30 years. Important educational reforms took place unifying Italian mid-school (1962) and liberalizing higher education attendance (1969). The Italian education reform process in 1989 was the first step towards the decentralisation of the university sector and the introduction of a general framework of didactic, organizational and scientific autonomy for all universities. This new reform took into account the principles of the Sorbonne Declaration (signed on 25th May 1998 by the Ministers of Education of 4 EU countries, namely France, Italy, Germany and the United Kingdom) and the Bologna Declaration. This declaration promoted the creation of a European Higher Education Area through the harmonisation of the different European educational systems. In 1999 almost all Italian universities were adapted to the Bologna process. Other milestones in education policy were the legislative decree 509/99,4, redefining the structure of the university system, and the 'Gelmini Reform' (Law 240/2010), changing the institutional governance and internal organization of Italian state universities. But Italy's higher education faced tumultuous time: as Monti (2008) stated in his investigation of the decline of the Italian university, more than 1,000 laws and rules were introduced from 1990 to 2006. Public policies regarding higher education allows to change (or rather permits changes) the system. Similar to Portugal and Spain, but in a slightly different timing, in Italy the growth of the university system which began after World War II reached a peak between 1980 and 2010, when the system virtually doubled in size. Italy experienced a remarkable increase in the numbers of students enrolled at university, percentages of 19-year-old students enrolled and number of graduations in the past 30 years (Turri 2014).

With a binary system, Italian higher education is organized in university (state and private universities, polytechnics, universities for foreigners, schools of advanced studies and on-line/distance learning universities) and non-university sector (among others, national academies in the Fine Arts, Cinema, Dance and Drama, Music Conservatories, schools and institutes for the education and training of professionals in various fields, such as language mediation, design, etc.).

Similar in timing and importance as in Portugal, Spain, and Italy, political and social changes took place in Greece in 1974. There also the country experienced a return to a democratic government and the admission to European Common Market in 1981. These were followed by changes in public policies on education, namely the Framework Law of 1982 (1268/82). In 1999, Greece accessed the Bologna Process. But comparing with other countries' progress, indicators on education showed Greece has undertaken almost all the commitments undertaken within the Bologna Process (Asderaki 2009).

The Greek higher education system grew. Themelis (2013) summarised the spectacular increase of Greek higher education: "Globally, between 1950 and 1970, tertiary-education enlargement was much higher than primary and secondary, with a net increase of approximately 300 percent. This trend continued unabated in the next 30 years. (...) This relevant statistics for Greece are even more startling. Between 1956 and 2001, the number of tertiary-education students grew nearly 16 times, while only between 1976 and 2001, the respective increase was fourfold. This rise, the second biggest among 31 European countries, makes Greece a remarkable case in Europe as far as educational expansion is concerned though not necessarily an exceptional one (HE participation between 1950 and 1965 more than doubles in almost every European country, with the exception of Spain and Portugal)" (Themelis 2013, p. 81–82).

As for Greece, the organization of higher education is a bit different as there are only public higher education institutions and private higher education is strictly forbidden. It comprises two parallel sectors: the university (Universities, Technical Universities, and the School of Fine Arts) and technological (Technological Education Institutions (TEIs) and the School of Pedagogical and Technological Education (ASPETE)) sectors. Greek higher education was developed according to a regional approach.

The structural and institutional transformations of these four countries along the last five to six decades results in profound reforms concerning education, where milestone public policies were implemented. There has been a gradual merging of higher education standards since the 1970s. Public policy reforms took place, including education broadly and higher education specifically. In summary, there is a consensus on identifying a significant growth of high literacy levels, a wider access to higher education in contrast to the previous elite university system, and education developing at an accelerate rate.

Despite singular differences in time and small details in structure, the four Mediterranean countries that have endured dictatorships were behind on the modernization process of higher education and society, compared to the Northern and Central Europe countries. These were countries with dictatorship regimes in the 1970s (and before) and with a transition to a democratic regime, influencing the way higher education reassumed a priority position. Before democratic times, higher education was in crisis, due to two reasons: a reduction in the university's autonomy to eliminate the production and free dissemination of critical thinking and authoritarian private projects competing with the university under unfair competition processes (Santos 2008). After that, the four countries' higher education systems moved on towards a stage of consolidation of mass higher education, following specific higher education policies towards a modern society and economy. In 1999 the Education Ministers of the four countries signed the Bologna Declaration and they began a general reform of higher education to move it towards the common European Higher Education Area (EHEA). The Bologna Process gave new impetus to the development of their national higher education systems (for a brief description of social changes and education, see Table 1).

Regarding political and social, and more specifically – what higher education is concerned with – processual similitude and coincidence in consequences, occurred in the four countries. However, this does not mean inner or even external homogeneity. The European Commission's guidelines and Europe 2020 goals tend to level EU members in education key indicators and benchmarks. So far it should be kept in mind each country's specificities, leading to a diversity of situations and higher education institutions. As van Vught et al. (2010) stated, diversity is "one of the major factors associated with the positive performance of higher education systems" (van Vught et al. 2010, p. 11), as diversity meets the needs of the labour market and reinforces the link and the role of higher education, economy and society, in another words, a market of university services (Santos 2008).

3 Data, methodologies and results

3.1 Data and Indicators about a Mediterranean higher education culture

Empirical data can help evaluate and measure the intensity of similitude and singularity between the four countries' experiences on higher education. Data was collected through reliable secondary sources with parameterized data: OECD, Eurostats, UNESCO-UIS.

In order to sustain and develop the previous reflection about the similitude of the four countries' higher education systems, some indicators were collected and analysed in a comparative way taking a longitudinal perspective. Some of those indicators are measuring the level of higher qualifications of the population in general and their level of employability, and others are referring to higher qualifications in specific sectors of the countries' economic activities. These indicators objectively measure the weighting higher education and qualified professions have in the construction and development of a modernization process of the society and the economy.

Table 1: Brief description of each country's Higher Education and recent socio-historical changes

	Greece	Italy	Portugal	Spain	Summary
Organization of HE	- University and technological - No private universities	- Binary system: university and non-university sector - Public and private	- 2 subsystems: university and polytechnic - Public and private	- University and non-university institutions - Public and private	→ Binary HE systems
Important changes in the country	- 1974: return to democratic government - EU in 1981	- After Fascist regime and WWII, 1946: Italian Republic - EU founding member	- After dictatorship, Revolution of 1974: democratic reform - EU in 1986	after dictatorship, 1978 Spanish Constitution - EU in 1986	→ Structural and institutional transformations
Public policies on Education	- Framework Law of 1982 (1268/82) and reform of higher education - 1999: the Bologna Process	- 1980 reform - Legislative decree no. 509/99,4 - 2015 La buona scuola	- LBSE 46/86 and 49/2005 - 1999: the Bologna Process	- University Reform Act of 1983 - Organic Law of Universities 2001 - 1999: the Bologna Process	→ Profound reforms in education
Consequences	- Five decades of reforms established high literacy levels	- From old elite university system to wider access	- Education developing at an accelerated rate	- Growth of tertiary education	→ Education and social changes

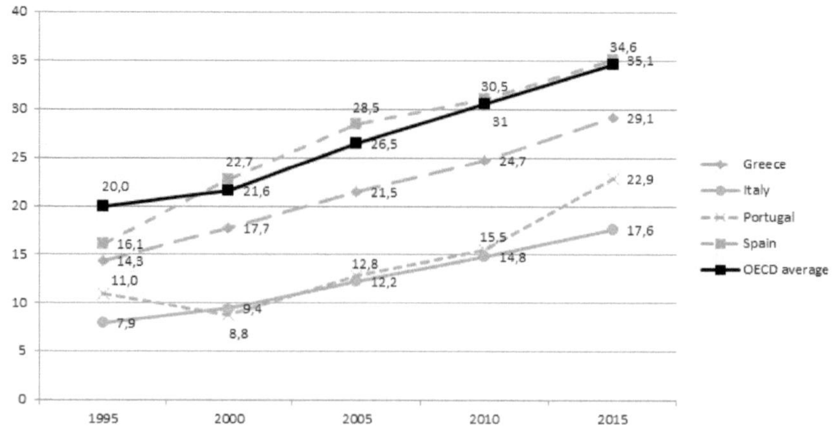

Source: Education at a glance: Educational attainment and labour-force status. OECD (2018), Adult education level (indicator). doi: https://doi.org/10.1787/36bce3fe-en (Accessed on 23 July 2018), International Standard Classification of Education (ISCED 2011 levels 5-8) http://uis.unesco.org/en/-topic/international-standard-classification-education-isced

Figure 1: Percentage of the 25-64-year-old population with tertiary education, 1995-2015

3.2 Results on a Mediterranean higher education culture

The indicator based on the share of population with tertiary education will be analysed in a longitudinal and comparative way. Since 1995, with intervals every five years until 2015, this information allows to see how much the importance of higher qualifications grew in the last two decades in each country.

As Figure 1 shows very clearly, in all four countries there is a considerable growth trend. Despite the growth in all of them, the comparison between the four countries shows different rhythms of growth: despite doubling or more in all of the four countries, it is lower in Italy and Portugal, while in Spain figures are quite impressive and quite similar to OECD average.

The importance of and investment in higher education clearly increased along generations: between middle 1990s and the most recent years, the percentage of young adults aged 25-34 with completed high qualifications almost doubled (Figure 2).

This growth is transversal to all four countries, but with some differences to highlight. Firstly, the percentage of young population with tertiary education in Spain has always been above the OECD average and the other three countries. This indicates a different investment levels, family culture, and the governments' policies towards higher education. Secondly, contradicting the general trend of continuous growth, in Spain there is a stabilization, if not a slight decrease, in the percentage of young people with higher education. Thirdly, the growth in the share of young people with higher education in Italy and in Portugal is even bigger if considering their low starting point in the middle 1990s, reflecting a tripling in two decades.

The growth of the percentage of highly qualified people is an effect of economic, social, political and cultural changes towards modernization, as education drives the modernization process. Holding a higher education degree should provide advantages in the labour market and in technology, industry and economy.

Finding employment after graduation is not the only indicator in the "higher education-labour market" relation: the adjustment between skills and competences provided by higher education and labour market needs, and adjustments to individual career changes are other pieces of the same puzzle that could be considered. However, by now the focus will be only on employment and unemployment rates by level of education.

According to recent OECD data, population's unemployment rates of people with higher qualifications vary from 19% in Greece, 6,8% in Italy, 8,2% in Portugal, and 12,4% Spain . All four countries are above the OECD average (4,8%).

Knowing that these percentages are in general lower for the graduated population than among less qualified people, the unemployment data must be read with caution as

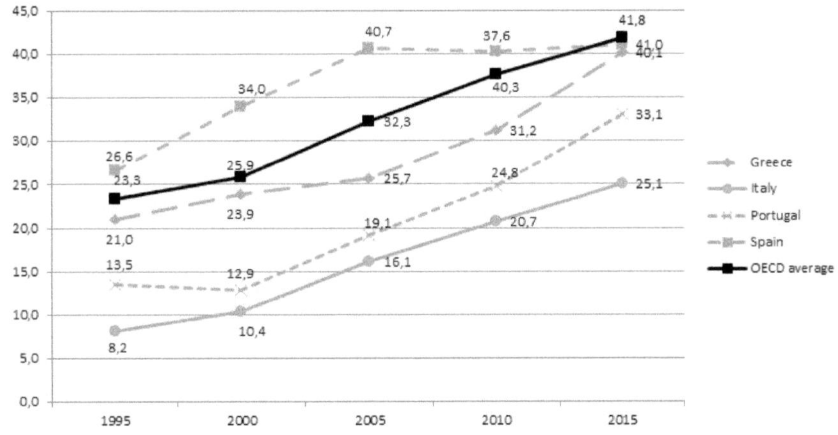

Source: Education at a glance: Educational attainment and labour-force status. OECD (2018), Population with tertiary education (indicator). doi: https://doi.org/10.1787/0b8f90e9-en (Accessed on 23 July 2018), International Standard Classification of Education (ISCED 2011 levels 5-8) http://uis.unesco.org/en/-topic/international-standard-classification-education-isced

Figure 2: Percentage of the 25-34-year-old population (% in the same age group) with tertiary education 1995-2015

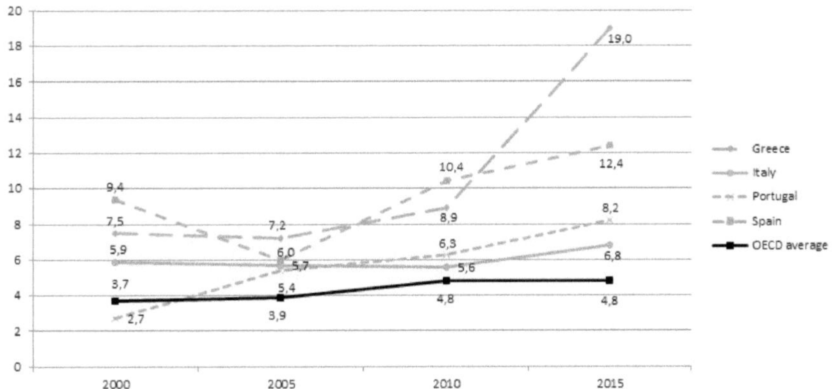

Source: OECD, International Standard Classification of Education (ISCED 2011 levels 5-8) http://uis.-unesco.org/en/topic/international-standard-classification-education-isced

Figure 3: Unemployment rates among population 25-64-years-old population with tertiary education 1995-2015

in these four Mediterranean countries external factors – and in particular the economic crisis – interfered in higher education attainment and in the capacity of the labour market recruiting high qualifications workforce, especially in the last decade (Figure 3).

The economic conjuncture affects the investment in education and training: for instance, in Italy, between 2009 and 2013, overall public funding for higher education was cut by approximately 20% in real terms (European Commission 2015). Governments' investment in higher education and in research and development are different in time, place and amount, which is an additional challenge in the comparison.

As Paleari et al. (2014) stated, because of the economic crisis, a withdrawal of the state as a financier happened in many countries, mainly in Southern Europe. New structures were built in order to respond to those changes. As Meek et al. (1991) stated, financial pressures appear to be driving higher education systems to change. But also the wish for higher education to be more closely tied to national economies (Meek et al. 1991), both in terms of meeting national labour market needs and through research discovering new products or resources, can produce changes in the higher education structure. That is why the percentage of highly qualified workforce in specific economic sectors is an interesting indicator to add to this analysis of a higher education culture.

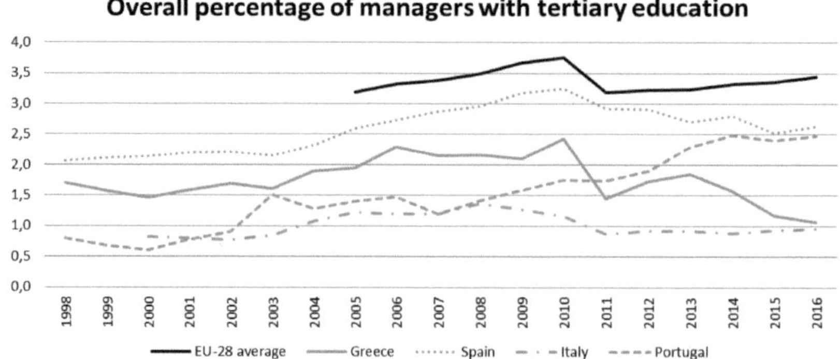

Source: Own calculations based on data from Eurostat on Employment by occupation and educational attainment level, International Standard Classification of Education (ISCED 2011 levels 5-8) http://uis.-unesco.org/en/topic/international-standard-classification-education-isced.

Figure 4: Overall percentage of managers with tertiary education among employed population 1998-2016

When specific occupations are considered in the analysis, the impact of the higher education growth is transferred to a change in the structure of qualified and unqualified employment. This change of the structure is understandable within a sociological perspective of a knowledge-based society (Krings 2006). Comparing the Southern European countries' higher education systems beyond the traditional figures on students and human resources involving higher education to describe its growth, the analysis aims to understand whether there is a shared common "higher education" culture in the Mediterranean countries.

The analysis combining economic indicators and higher education indicators will be essential to validate this interesting perspective. Data on employment and on levels of education (according to ISCED 2011 classification) will now be considered: in particular, data on the percentage of higher education qualifications in specific occupations, such as managers, professionals, and technicians and associate professionals, according to the ISCO 2008 classification (ILO 2012).

The analysis is supported using Eurostat data between 1995 and 2016 (the most recent data) and comparing the four Southern Europe Mediterranean countries with the EU-28 average. Despite the relation between these four countries and the EU being historically and culturally different, the option of using EU-28 average allows an ongoing comparison including all EU members instead of focusing only on the "classic" EU-15. Besides, differences between EU-28 and EU-15 trends are small.

Overall, the percentage of managers with tertiary education is around 3,5% in EU-28 countries. In the four Mediterranean countries, this score is lower; between 1,0% in Italy and Greece and around 2,5% in Spain and Portugal in the most recent year (Figure 4). Despite this difference, in all of them there is a growing trend in having more managers with higher qualifications managers: since the beginning of the last decade, in Spain it surpasses 50% of managers with higher education (Figure 5). However, the lack of higher qualifications of the executives and managers still remains a thorn in the structure of the labour market.

It is among professionals (according to the ISCO 2008 classification) that the presence of higher qualifications is unquestionable and has been increasing each decade: in 2005 qualified professionals were around 11% in a EU-28 average, above that in Greece and Spain, and around 8% in Italy and Portugal (Figure 6). In ten years this figure grew around 50% on average in Europe and in all of the Mediterranean countries except in Portugal, where it more than doubled. changing the structure of the labour market and its qualifications. Furthermore, in Spain, Greece and Portugal, more than 90% of the professionals have a higher education diploma, while the EU-28 average is some percentage points lower (Figure 7).

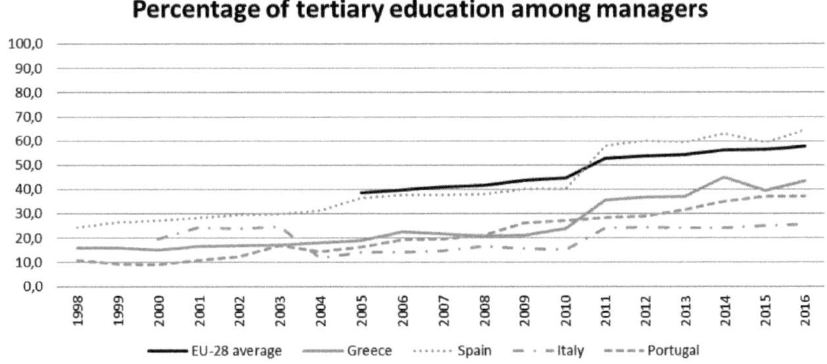

Source: Own calculations based on data from Eurostat on Employment by occupation and educational attainment level, International Standard Classification of Education (ISCED 2011 levels 5-8) http://uis.-unesco.org/en/topic/international-standard-classification-education-isced.

Figure 5: Percentage of managers with tertiary education among managers 1998-2016

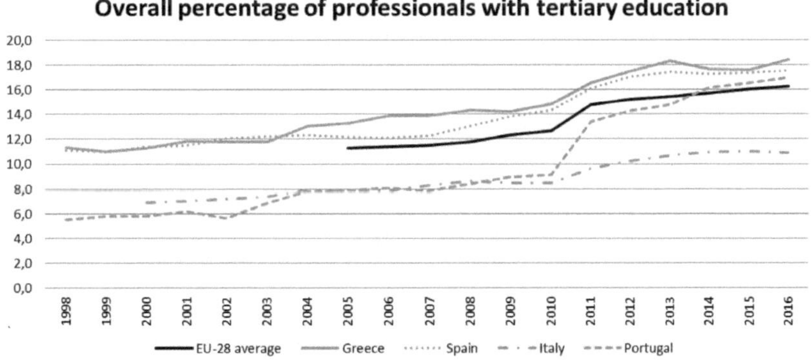

Source: Own calculations based on data from Eurostat on Employment by occupation and educational attainment level, International Standard Classification of Education (ISCED 2011 levels 5-8) http://uis.-unesco.org/en/topic/international-standard-classification-education-isced.

Figure 6: Overall percentage of professionals with tertiary education among employed population 1998-2016

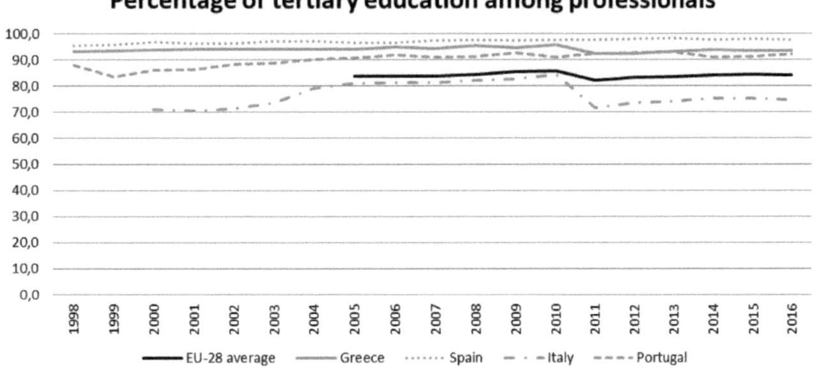

Source: Own calculations based on data from Eurostat on Employment by occupation and educational attainment level, International Standard Classification of Education (ISCED 2011 levels 5-8) http://uis.-unesco.org/en/topic/international-standard-classification-education-isced.

Figure 7: Percentage of professionals with tertiary education among professionals 1998-2016

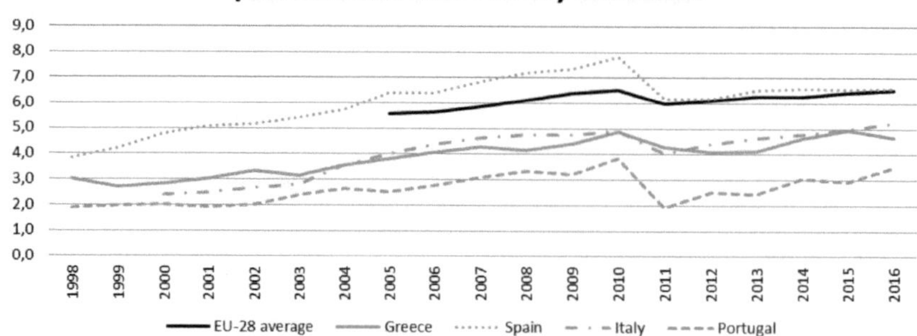

Source: Own calculations based on data from Eurostat on Employment by occupation and educational attainment level, International Standard Classification of Education (ISCED 2011 levels 5-8) http://uis.unesco.org/en/topic/international-standard-classification-education-isced.

Figure 8: Overall percentage of technicians and associate professionals with tertiary education among employed population 1998-2016

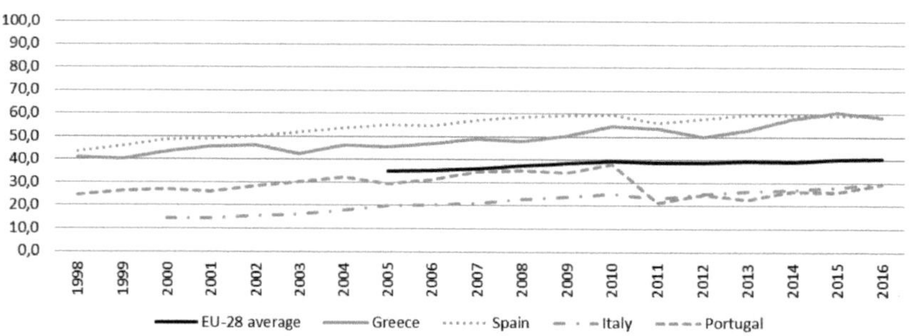

Source: Own calculations based on data from Eurostat on Employment by occupation and educational attainment level, International Standard Classification of Education (ISCED 2011 levels 5-8) http://uis.unesco.org/en/topic/international-standard-classification-education-isced.

Figure 9: Percentage of technicians and associate professionals with tertiary education among technicians and associate professionals 1998-2016

The increase of technicians and associate professionals in the labour market is also a reality, although at a slower place and in a different proportion when comparing to managers and professionals.

Again, Spain is particularly paradigmatic of these growing trends, reinforcing the relation between: higher education and the economy, the labour market and modernity, as well as technology and innovation (Figure 8). In Spain and Greece, technicians with high qualifications are actually greater than 50% of the workforce, while the average in EU-28 is around 40%. In Portugal and Italy the share is about 10% less than the EU-8 average (Figure 9).

Deepening the analysis on the relation between higher qualifications and the economy using Eurostat data from 2008 onwards on technology and knowledge-intensive sectors' employment, NACE classification (European Commission 2008) at the national level will be used. This will be used to consider the percentage of workers with tertiary education. It is also a way to evaluate how far higher education is part of the engine of modernizing the economy and the society.

Krings (2006), based on Reich (1991, cited by Krings (2006)), mentions the importance of "symbolic" work, by creating a visible spectrum of knowledge-based activities: production knowledge (research and development, innovation and market oriented products);

targeting knowledge (administration, management, organisation); and orientation knowledge (consulting, controlling, co-ordination), as well as the importance of knowledge-based technology for the political decision making process and public service sector, and the importance of a new professional class with a specific professional profile (technology and knowledge based).

Comparing the percentage of highly qualified workers in different sectors in the four countries and taking the EU-28 average as a reference, it is by far the Services sector that absorbs the majority of the graduated workforce: more than 80% of the workers in that sector hold a higher education diploma. This is particularly evident in Greece, Portugal and Italy, rather than in Spain. The second and third most important sectors in recruiting highly qualified workforce are Education (especially in Greece and Portugal) and Human health and social work activities (especially in Italy and Portugal). Among all the other sectors, three sectors can be highlighted by having around 10% of graduated workforce: Manufacturing (but with lower percentages in Greece and Portugal), Wholesale and retail trade (but with higher values in Greece and in Spain) and Professional, scientific and technical activities (and with 6% more in Italy).

Technological advances and the requirement of more sophisticated skills, have both contributed to changes in the work structure across the world and increased the demand for higher-education graduates (Antonowicz 2012). Limiting the analysis to high-technology sectors, the average in EU-28 is around 7%. In Greece and Portugal it is slightly lower.

The knowledge economy and knowledge-based industries development is marked by the growing demand for higher-education graduates to drive this dynamic sector of the European economy (Antonowicz 2012). Selecting some of the sectors involving high-technology, it is quite remarkable the concentration of qualified workers in knowledge-intensive high technology services when comparing, for instance, with high and medium high-technology manufacturing. And it is particularly evident in other knowledge-intensive market services except financial intermediation and high-technology services. It occurs less in Spain, when comparing with the other countries and with EU-28 average (Table 2).

4   Discussion and Concluding Remarks

The main concern of this article is reflecting and analysing the similarities or differences between Mediterranean countries' higher education and its relation to the labour market. Related, how linked they are to a possible Mediterranean way of thinking and substantiate a common higher education culture. Based on similar historical, social, political, and economic background – and often their developments aligning temporally – the changes in the four countries' higher education followed the same trend.

Higher education in Portugal, Greece, Spain and Italy can be characterised by a similitude of growing importance as a core value in the society, in a time coincidence of changing in political, economic and social dimensions in the last four decades. Significant structural changes have been made in the educational systems, with is clearly reflected in tertiary education. In these countries' second moment, the admission to the European Union and the adaptation of the higher education system to Bologna's guidelines also contributed to a fast, wider and remarkable consolidation of higher education in each society and each economy.

The implementation of the Bologna Process makes it difficult to identify the similitude behind the structure European higher education systems should follow. As Gilder, Wells (2009) suggested, little consideration has been given to the content of each level's qualification and their fitness for purpose (e.g. areas relevant to the labour market). Even before the EU and the Bologna process, the four countries' higher education trajectory is quite similar. However, the lack of adjustment highlighted in some Southern European countries, despite of their improved convergence toward the EU-15 average, can be explained by the deficit of modernization theory (and relevant policy) to address structural problems of countries and regions. For example, lack of quality governance, path dependency, and cultural diversity. In a certain way, a first important conclusion of this study is the confirmation of a Mediterranean higher education culture, which is reflected in their changes. Most of these trends are linked to an effort of modernization of

Table 2: Percentage of workers with tertiary education in NACE (Rev.2) sectors and in NACE high-technology sectors, 2008 and 2016

	EU-28		GR		SP		IT		PT	
	2008	2016	2008	2016	2008	2016	2008	2016	2008	2016
in all activities	26.8	33.9	26.3	35.1	33.9	42.1	17.0	21.3	15.1	26.3
in Agriculture, forestry and fishing; mining and quarrying	1.5	1.5	1.1	1.8	1.3	1.3	0.8	0.9	1.2	1.1
in Manufacturing	11.5	10.6	6.4	6.1	12.3	10.5	8.3	9.2	6.3	7.8
in Electricity, gas, steam and air conditioning supply; water supply and construction	5.2	4.7	2.9	2.5	7.1	4.6	2.4	2.2	4.0	3.2
in Wholesale and retail trade; accomodation and food service activities; activities of households as employers	10.5	11.6	13.8	16.0	15.1	16.8	9.0	10.1	10.1	12.2
in Land transport, transport via pipelines, water transport, air transport, warehousing and support activities for transportation; travel agency, tour operator reservation services and related activities	2.6	2.7	2.3	3.9	3.2	3.5	1.7	1.7	1.6	2.4
in Services	81.5	82.6	89.6	89.6	79.3	83.6	88.5	87.6	88.5	88.0
in Information and communication	5.3	5.6	2.7	4.0	5.8	5.5	4.6	4.5	4.6	5.2
in Financial and insurance activities; real estate activities	5.6	5.7	5.4	4.4	5.6	5.3	5.2	5.5	6.4	6.3
in Professional, scientific and technical activities	10.1	11.0	14.2	12.5	9.9	10.1	17.0	17.1	12.1	11.1
in Administrative and support service activities	2.5	2.8	1.2	1.5	2.7	3.0	2.4	2.3	1.7	2.2
in Public administration; activities of extraterritorial organisations and bodies	9.8	9.2	14.6	13.6	9.0	8.7	8.1	7.1	8.7	7.6
in Education	16.9	15.8	22.7	20.4	14.2	14.2	20.2	17.4	27.5	21.5
in Human health and social work activities	14.0	13.9	10.6	10.8	10.9	12.6	16.9	17.9	13.2	15.6
in Arts, entertainment and recreation	2.1	2.2	1.4	1.5	1.8	2.2	1.7	2.2	1.3	2.3
in Other activities services	2.1	2.1	1.1	1.2	1.8	1.9	1.8	1.8	1.3	1.6
in NACE high-technology and or knowledge-intensive sectors	7.0	7.1	3.9	4.6	6.6	6.8	6.3	6.5	5.9	5.5
in High and medium high-technology manufacturing	5.8	5.5	1.7	1.8	4.9	4.7	4.1	4.8	2.7	2.7
in Knowledge-intensive services	64.0	63.5	72.2	69.3	57.1	58.8	73.9	71.7	73.7	69.6
in Knowledge-intensive high-technology services	5.4	5.7	3.0	3.6	5.8	5.7	4.9	4.8	4.3	5.3
in Knowledge-intensive market services (except financial intermediation and high-technology services)	10.1	11.0	14.2	14.1	10.2	10.2	16.2	16.4	12.1	10.9
in Financial and insurance activities	4.8	4.8	5.3	4.3	4.8	4.5	4.9	4.9	5.6	5.4
in Other knowledge-intensive market services (except financial intermediation and high-technology services)	43.8	42.1	49.7	47.4	36.3	38.4	48.0	45.6	51.7	48.0

Source: Own calculations based on data from Eurostat on Employment in technology and knowledge-intensive NACE Rev. 2 sectors at the national level, by level of education, International Standard Classification of Education (ISCED 2011 levels 5-8) http://uis.unesco.org/en/topic/international-standard-classification-education-isced.

the societies and national economies, in a strong relation to the structure of the labour market at a national and transnational level.

As Meek et al. (1991) stated (and is still valid), many national systems of higher education have been experiencing profound changes by being asked to participate more effectively and efficiently in producing a better educated, culturally enriched, and more economically secure society. Therefore, reinforcing the relation between higher education and the labour market.

Reforms frequently express a path-dependent nature, and every higher education system reflects country-specific regulatory and coordination regimes. This also largely reflect national historical and institutional developments, as each national system is embedded into its own regulations and bears nuances and peculiarities (Donina et al. 2015). And that is why along with some similitude, diversity and singularities can be found, due to different policies, political and economic strategies, as well as different relations between higher education and sectors of the economy.

By analysing data, it seems clear the existence of similitudes between the national systems despite the different shades which are observed from country to country. It was possible to conclude from this exploratory analysis that all four countries have been trying to catch up to the EU average in terms of population's qualification. This was less evident in Spain, where the percentage is even above the EU-28 average. Additionally, this catch up can be observed in the employment of graduates despite still having lower percentages comparing to EU.

Comparing to the EU-28, the current position of each country in educational indicators and their link to labour market indicators is quite similar, in spite of some nuances. Among the four, Spain is the most divergent.

When specific occupations or activity sectors are taken into account, singularities between the four countries emerge, while other similitude persist. In all four, the qualifications of managers and executives are below the EU average; also, Services is where most qualified workforce are. Some singularities, such as less qualified professionals in Italy or less qualified technicians in Italy and Portugal, might be a consequence (or a cause) of a different structure of the economy and industry. Furthermore, differences in some activity sectors and in particular those related to high-technology knowledge intense services might occur either by the structure of the demand of study programmes in each country or by the structure of the needs of the labour market. Much of the singularities depend on other factors affecting the relation between higher education and the labour market on a regional and local level. These conclusions can guide future analysis deepening the focus on a regional level, taking into account different weights of high qualified workforce and different technologic sectors. At the same time, the conclusions also reinforce the strength of regional developments in the economic and social sustainability of societies. Newland writes, "universities have the potential to make an enormous contribution to regional development" (Newlands 2003, p. 15). However, as "regional economic development policy and practice are multi-layered with universities involved at different levels and in different roles" (Newlands 2003, p. 15), further analysis should be focused on a regional dimension of the relation between higher education and labour market, differentiating dominant regions from others (Angelis et al. 2016), in each of the four countries.

Other factors – internal and/or external – that weren't controlled in this study might be interfering. One of those might be the population's demographic structure: as Sprague (2016) suggested, reform of higher education should take into account the trend of ageing and depopulation, given their significant implications for higher education policy. Such reforms include increasing adaptability and employability of the labour force, and participation of the population in the labour market. Also migration is an important and not considered factor. Specifically the phenomenon of brain-drain, where people leave their 'home' country for another country in pursuit of tertiary education. In our globalized labour market, this might be a hypothesis for some maladjustment between higher education and employment in some countries.

Another important question is, in which way education and higher education is defined as part and parcel of each country's strategy for economic development. And this depends quite often on political programmes, political-party's leanings, and the back and forth of the political pendulum.

Comparing and confronting other groups of European countries, the conclusions on similitude are reinforced. Thus, it is unanimous that higher education has been and still is a core value in all of the four countries as universities will be the cultural reference points for their communities, will have an essential role as a social institution, and will contribute to establishing local social dynamics (Paleari et al. 2014). As Zuti and Lukovics argue, "universities are able to positively contribute to the competitiveness of their regions by considering strategic thinking and third mission activities with the help of tools of economic development" (Zuti, Lukovics 2015, p. 29). This is particularly important for a micro- and meso-perspective, and considering regional contexts. This research has furthered an understanding of strategic considerations for regional development with regards to the inter-relation between economic sectors, the labour market and higher education.

Acknowledgement

This article is based on some preliminary reflections on higher education systems in Europe, integrated in the author's post-doctoral research project on non-university (polytechnic) system in Portugal and the relations between public policies, the educational offer and the social and economic context. This research is supported by Fundação para a Ciência e a Tecnologia (FCT/MCTES) – grant SFRH/BPD/110394/2015 – and this article was made with the support of CICS.NOVA – Interdisciplinary Centre of Social Sciences of the Universidade Nova de Lisboa, UID/SOC/04647/2013, with the financial support of FCT/MCTES through National funds.

This reflection on similitudes and singularities of higher education systems follows the International Centre for Studies and Research (ICSR) Mediterranean Knowledge and the Research Centre for Spatial and Organizational Dynamics (CIEO) invitation to participate in the 2nd International Conference ICSR Mediterranean Knowledge – Faro, Portugal, 2017, about "Mediterranean Cultures and Societies – Knowledge, Health and Tourism", on the topic Knowledge and educational processes.

References

Angelis V, Angelis-Dimakis A, Dimaki K (2016) Identifying Clusters of Regions in the European South, based on their Economics, Social and Environmental Characteristics. *REGION* 3[2]: 71–102. CrossRef.

Antonowicz D (2012) Europe 2050. New Europeans and Higher Education. In: Kwiek M, Kurkiewicz A (eds), *The Modernisation of European Universities*. Peter Lang 113-127, Frankfurt. CrossRef.

Asderaki F (2009) The Impact of the Bologna Process on the Development of the Greek Quality Assurance System. *Quality in Higher Education* 15[2]: 105–122. CrossRef.

Birnbaum R (1983) *Maintaining Diversity in Higher Education*. Jossey-Bass, San Francisco

Clark BR (1973) Development of the Sociology of Higher Education. *Sociology of Education* 6[1]: 2–14. CrossRef.

Díaz JI (2010) La reforma de los planes de estudio universitarios de la España democrática (1977-2000). *Revista de Educación* 351: 259–282

Deleuze G (1990) *The logic of sense*. Columbia University Press, New York

Donina D, Meoli M, Paleari S (2015) Higher Education Reform in Italy: Tightening regulation instead of steering at a distance. *Higher Education Policy* 28[2]: 215–234. CrossRef.

Drucker P (1969) *The Age of Discontinuity*. Harper and Row, New York

European Comission (2017) Communication from the Commission to the European Parliament, the Council, the European Economic and Social Committee and the Committee of the Regions – on a renewed EU agenda for higher education. Com(2017) 247 final. https://eur-lex.europa.eu/legal-content/EN/TXT/PDF/?.uri=-CELEX:52017DC0247&from=DA

European Commission (2008) NACE Rev. 2. Statistical classification of economic activities in the European Community. Luxembourg: Office for Official Publications of the European Communities. http://ec.europa.eu/eurostat/documents/3859598/5902521/KS-RA-07-015-EN.PDF/dd5443f5-b886-40e4-920d-9df03590ff91?.version=1.0

European Commission (2015) Education and training monitor 2015 Italy. Luxembourg, Publications Office of the European Union. http://ec.europa.eu/dgs/education_culture/repository/education/tools/docs/2015/monitor2015-italy_en.pdf. CrossRef.

Foucault M (1983) *This Is Not a Pipe*. University of California Press, Berkely

Gambarotto F, Solari S (2014) The peripheralization of Southern European capitalism within the MEU. *Review of International Political Economy* 22[4]: 788–812. CrossRef.

Gilder E, Wells PJ (2009) Bologna "unplugged": Uncovering the base track of a major European-wide higher educational reform initiative. *American, British and Canadian Studies* 12: 114–131

Hook D (2007) *Foucault, Psychology and the Analytics of Power*. Palgrave MacMillan, London. CrossRef.

ILO – International Labour Organization (2012) ISCO – International Standard Classification of Occupations. Geneva: ILO. http://www.ilo.org/public/english/bureau/stat/-isco/isco08/

Katrougalos G, Lazaridis G (2003) *Southern European Welfare States: Problems, Challenges and Prospects*. Palgrave MacMillan, New York. CrossRef.

Kivinen O, Nurmi J (2003) Unifying higher education for different kinds of Europeans. Higher education and work: A comparison of ten countries. *Comparative Education* 39[1]: 83–103. CrossRef.

Krings B (2006) The sociological perspective on the knowledge-based society: Assumptions, facts and visions. MPRA Paper no. 7110. http://mpra.ub.uni-muenchen.de/7110/

Lazaridis G (1996) Southern Europe in transition. *Journal of Area Studies* 4[9]: 6–16. CrossRef.

Maassen PA (1996) The concept of Culture and Higher Education. *Tertiary Education and Management* 1[2]: 153–159. CrossRef.

Meek V, Goedegebuure LC, Kivinen O, Rinne R (1991) Policy change in higher education – Intended and unintended outcomes. *Higher Education* 21: 451–459. CrossRef.

Mitchell DE, Nielsen SY (2012) Internationalization and globalization in higher education. In: Cuadra-Montiel H (ed), *Globalization - Education and Management Agendas*. InTech. http://cdn.intechopen.com/pdfs/38270/InTech-Internationalization_and_globalization_in_higher_education.pdf, London

Monti A (2008) *Indagine sul declino dell'università italiana*. Gangemi Editore, Rome

Newlands D (2003) The role of universities in learning regions. 43rd congress of the European Regional Science Association, European Regional Science Association. https://-www.econstor.eu/bitstream/10419/116149/1/ERSA2003_398.pdf

Paleari S, Donina D, Meoli M (2014) The role of the university in twenty-first century European society. *The Journal of Technology Transfer* 40[3]: 369–379. CrossRef.

Piris J (2012) *The Future of Europe: Towards a Two-Speed EU?* Cambridge University Press, Cambridge. CrossRef.

Reich R (1991) *The Work of Nations. Preparing Ourselves for 21st-Century Capitalism.* Knopf, New York

Roncevic B (2001) Path from the (semi)periphery to the core: On the role of socio-cultural factors. IES Proceedings 1.1. http://www.ies.ee/iesp/roncevic.pdf

Santiago P, Brunner JJ, Haug G, Malo S, di Pietrogiacomoet P (2009) Spain. OECD Reviews of Tertiary Education. https://www.oecd.org/spain/42309226.pdf

Santos BS (2008) *A universidade no século XXI: para uma reforma democrática e emancipatória da universidade.* Edições Afrontamento, Porto

Sprague T (2016) *Education in Non-EU Countries in Western and Southern Europe.* Bloomsbury Academic, New York. CrossRef.

Stamelos G, Paivandi S (2015) Access to higher education in Southern Europe. *Academia* 5[1]: 1–17

Subirats J (2001) Universidad en España: ¿época de cambios o cambio de época? *Educar* 28: 11–39

Teichler U (2007) *Higher education systems: Conceptual frameworks, comparative perspectives, empirical Findings.* Sense Publishers, Rotterdam and Taipei

Themelis S (2013) *Social Change and Education in Greece: A Study in Class Struggle Dynamics.* Palgrave Macmillan, London

Turri M (2014) The difficult transition of the Italian university system: Growth, underfunding and reforms. *Journal of Further and Higher Education* 40[1]: 83–106. CrossRef.

UNESCO (1998) Higher Education in the twenty-first Century Vision and Action, Volume 1, Final Report. World Conference on Higher Education. Paris

van Vught FA, Kaiser F, File J, Gaethgens C, Peter R, Westerheijden D (2010) The European Classification of Higher Education Institutions. Enschede: CHEPS. http://www.u-map.eu/U-MAP_report.pdf

Vanhercke B, Natali D, Bouget D (2016) Social policy in the European Union: State of play 2016. Brussels: European Trade Union Institute (ETUI) and European Social Observatory (OSE)

Villarroya A, Hernández M, Llopis R, Navarro P, Tejerina B (2008) *El Oficio de Estudiar en la Universidad: compromisos flexibles.* PUV (Publicacions de la Universitat de València), Valencia

Wallerstein I (1979) *The Capitalist World Economy.* Cambridge University Press, New York. CrossRef.

Waters M (1995) *Globalization.* Routledge, London

Williams A (1984) *Southern Europe Transformed: Political and economic change in Greece, Italy, Portugal and Spain.* Harper and Row, London

Zuti B, Lukovics M (2015) "Fourth Generation" Universities and Regional Development. In: Hamm R, Kopper J (eds), *Higher Education Institutions and Regional Development Proceedings of the 3rd ERSA International Workshop.* Stünings Medien, Krefeld, 14–31

REGION

The Journal of ERSA
Powered by WU

Volume 5, Number 1, 2018, 101–112
DOI: 10.18335/region.v5i1.219

journal homepage: region.ersa.org

The Mediterranean Diet and the Increasing Demand of the Olive Oil Sector: Shifts and Environmental Consequences

Bruno Neves[1], Iva Miranda Pires[1]

[1] Universidade Nova de Lisboa, Lisbon, Portugal

Received: 29 September 2017/Accepted: 13 May 2018

Abstract. Mediterranean countries play a crucial role as olive oil producers and consumers compared to other world regions. In particular, the Northern Mediterranean countries, where Spain, Italy, Greece and Portugal alone represent 68% of the world's olive oil production and 43% of world consumption. Nevertheless, aspects such as communication with emphasis on the benefits of the Mediterranean diet - which is a distinctive characteristic of the Mediterranean culture and identity and where olive oil plays an important role - the Slow Food Movement, the International Olive Council campaigns, and the successive Common Agricultural Policies, have triggered production, trade and consumption around the world. Such increases and stimuli brought and are still bringing changes to the olive oil sector such as a shifting tendency in production modes as well as modernization of the sector and new plantations, in response to consumers' increasing demand. But these shifts are creating a paradoxical situation in the sense that the promotion of a healthier diet is having a perverse environmental effect as the production of olive oil is shifting to more intensive production systems and monoculture plantations which are changing landscapes and are referred to as environmentally harmful to the ecosystems. These issues are here debated and illustrated with case study examples, referring to the Mediterranean countries, particularly in the Iberian Peninsula.

JEL classification: Q18

Key words: Agricultural Policies, Environment, Mediterranean Diet, Olive Oil

1 Introduction

The Mediterranean Diet plays an important role in Mediterranean societies given the large scope of its meaning and what it represents. Its relevance led to a joint application from multiple Mediterranean countries, comprising Cyprus, Croatia, Spain, Greece, Italy, Morocco and Portugal, to submit a nomination to the United Nations Educational, Scientific and Cultural Organization (UNESCO) for the recognition of the Mediterranean Diet as Intangible Cultural Heritage of Humanity.

As it can be read on the Nomination File No. 00884 from UNESCO (2013b), the Mediterranean Diet is a way of life, involving a set of skills, knowledge, rituals, symbols and traditions, and it respects crops, harvesting, picking, fishing, animal husbandry, conservation, processing, cooking and, foremost, the act of sharing and eating the traditional cuisine together at a table, where knowledge floats from generation to generation. It encompasses a strong social sense transposed to the cultural spaces, festivals and other celebrations associated to the Mediterranean, emphasizing values of mutual recognition and respect, hospitality, neighborliness, conviviality, intergenerational transmission and intercultural dialogue.

The Mediterranean Diet was inscribed on the Representative List of the Intangible Cultural Heritage of Humanity, a decision that was made during the Eighth Session of the Intergovernmental Committee (8.COM) held in Baku, Azerbaijan, from Monday 2nd to Saturday 7th December 2013, and can be read on the "Decisions" document, released with all decisions taken at the 8.COM, namely the Decision 8.COM 8.10 concerning to the Mediterranean Diet (UNESCO 2013a, p. 36-37).

This recognition of the Mediterranean Diet by UNESCO highlighting the above-mentioned aspects gives it a broader range and influence not only in the region itself but worldwide. The benefits of the Mediterranean Diet have also been recognized by other institutions such as the Food and Agriculture Organization (FAO) of the United Nations, the International Olive Council (IOC), and the European Union, amongst others.

If UNESCO recognized added value in the Mediterranean Diet through its set of skills, knowledge, practices and traditions, the FAO recognition was more concerned to its relevancy to greener economies and development in regions of small-scale tourism and agriculture. Such recognition was previously highlighted by FAO through the inclusion of the Mediterranean Diet in the group of the most sustainable diets in 2012 (Moro 2016), which is defined as *"those diets with low environmental impacts which contribute to food and nutrition security and to a healthy life for present and future generations. Sustainable diets are protective and respectful of biodiversity and ecosystems, culturally acceptable, accessible, economically fair and affordable; nutritionally adequate, safe and healthy; while optimizing natural and human resources"* (FAO 2010, p. 7).

Other institutions highlight food products associated to the Mediterranean Diet that may be referred to in groups, representing a pyramid of the optimal Mediterranean Diet or mentioned as a list (Huang, Sumpio 2008).

The IOC website has a webpage dedicated to the "Mediterranean Diet Pyramid" and the food products are presented by categories in a descending order of recommended quantity and frequency. The classification is presented as follows: (i) grains (bread, pasta, couscous and rice); (ii) fruits and vegetables (in-season products. Fruits eaten as dessert); (iii) legumes and nuts (chickpeas, lentils, haricot beans, pine kernels, almonds, hazelnuts, walnuts); (iv) olive oil and olives; (v) dairy products (cheese, yoghurt and other dairy products, although milk is not specially mentioned), and; (vi) fish (seen as first-class protein). On the top level of the pyramid, and therefore, the least advised food products, are red meat, sweets and pastries. Wine (preferably red) is advised to be consumed with moderation during meals and no more than two glasses per day (IOC nd). Out of the food products, regular physical activity is also recommended (Huang, Sumpio 2008, IOC nd).

In literature when food products related to Mediterranean Diet are mentioned, often health benefits are revealed, forming an inseparable association (Huang, Sumpio 2008, Pires, Neves 2013). In Moro (2016), Mediterranean Diet is described as a "healthy system of living and feeding" along with a list of food products similar to the above listed. Huang, Sumpio (2008) refer to the inhabitants of the involving regions surrounding the North and South of the Mediterranean Sea to have a longer life expectancy and lower risk of chronic diseases, in comparison with other world regions. Mediterranean Populations' diet and lifestyle are believed to have led to decreased rates of cancer, diabetes and heart diseases.

Independently of the scope of institutions or sources of information about Mediterranean Diet (e.g. cultural, social, environmental, health, and food products) in this paper we are focusing on olive oil, the fat (of choice) associated with the Mediterranean Diet.

The olive oil market is characterized by a period of considerable stability during the 1970s, a situation that would change in the following decades. In the 1980s, the olive oil sector registered a growth due to changes introduced in dietary patterns and increasing demand in non-producing countries, an answer that had to be given by producing countries. Despite the increasing and continued demand registered since the 1980s, it is the shifting to the 21st century that sets a breaking point in which olive oil shifted from being an expensive niche commodity to an everyday product. These changes became evident and acquired more visibility in Europe. Food stores started having more brands and varieties of olive oil than other cooking or edible oils, reducing their importance in the market (Neves, Pires 2013, Scheidel, Krausmann 2011).

The next section discusses how communication emphasizing the benefits of the Mediterranean Diet in general, and olive oil in particular, the Slow Food Movement and campaigns such as those being promoted by the IOC, and the successive Common Agricultural Policies (CAP) have been stimulating an increasing demand and subsequently changing the olive oil industry and its practices towards intensive and super-intensive modes of production in order to meet that demand. Then, in the following session, we discuss how those stimuli have been environmentally undermined and we illustrate those situations with Iberian Peninsula case study examples.

2   Olive Oil Stimuli in a changing Industry

2.1   The International Olive Council campaigns

Olive oil has been part of the populations' diets in the Mediterranean region for thousands of years (de Graaff et al. 2008), its advantages being well known, scientifically studied and proved. It has been presented as a healthy natural product that contributes to a more balanced diet, a fundamental good that contributes to a healthier lifestyle (Neves, Pires 2013, Pires, Neves 2013).

The marketing generated around olive oil would, in fact, take over the healthy tags linked to olive oil and supported by the benefits of the Mediterranean Diet. It followed the wine industry, presenting fine design of bottles and creative labels introducing gourmet versions for high-end segments, such as extra virgin olive oils (Pires, Neves 2013).

Founded in 1959, with the objective to support and promote the olive oil production, trade and consumption, the IOC saw its objective accomplished by emphasizing precisely the health benefits of olive oil. Back then the underlined health benefits were associated with anti-aging, cardiovascular diseases, pregnancy and obesity (Huang, Sumpio 2008, Scheidel, Krausmann 2011). With a total budget of approximately 10 million Euros, IOC was spending half of its budget in promoting olive oil worldwide (Scheidel, Krausmann 2011).

In 1986, the European Union started to support the IOC with an annual budget of five million Euros, that lasted until 2002 and was considerably reduced afterwards to half a million (Scheidel, Krausmann 2011).

2.2   The European Union campaigns

Even though the "partnership" between IOC and EU dates from 1986, the EU promotion campaigns started earlier. In 1981, the EU was starting olive oil promotional campaigns only in producing countries. The objective at that time was clear, to replace other edible oils, commonly designated as cheaper, in the market by olive oil. In 1991 the EU widened its campaigns to non-producing countries, and, as it was already mentioned, since 1986, the EU was co-funding the IOC promotional campaigns (Scheidel, Krausmann 2011). According to the same authors, it is estimated that the total amount spent in olive oil campaigns from 1985 to 2002 exceeded 150 million Euros.

Around this time, the campaigns started shifting their messages, indicating a change in objectives and ultimately the discourse around olive oil. The goal was no longer to replace other oils in the market but instead to promote olive oil as a healthy commodity in line with the Mediterranean Diet benefits discourse. Despite the scientific basis supporting these EU campaigns and highlighting the health benefits of olive oil, it was not consensual, and therefore, there were some critics around the motto of the campaigns (Scheidel, Krausmann 2011).

2.2.1 The Common Agricultural Policy (CAP) campaigns

Within the CAP there were two periods worth mentioning: the 1998 CAP reform, initially set from 1998 to 2001, and extended until 2004, in which the EU was supporting products and producers through market-based policies, and at the same time, improving production systems and infrastructures through structural policies. In 2003, the EU introduced a PAC reform with the main objectives of encouraging productivity, market stabilization and protecting rural livelihoods (De Gennaro et al. 2012, de Graaff et al. 2011, Scheidel, Krausmann 2011, Stoate et al. 2009).

The first trend of market based policies was justified by the relevance of olive oil production and consumption in specified regions and was thus provided as aid to production and consumption. Along with it came price support and trade barriers imposed on third countries, avoiding cheap olive oil imports. As a result, the large amounts of aid provided by CAP led to an increase and intensification of the olive oil sector, being this aid proportional to the amount of olive oil produced. Production aid was initially set to last from 1998 until 2001, however, the Regulation Nr. 1513/2001 of the European Community extended it until 2004. With the end of the production aid, new mandatory environmental rules were introduced to agricultural practices. These changes reflected environmental concerns related to further intensification in production modes and it was expected that such measures would reduce the erosion rates that arose, a consequence of such reforms (European Commission 2003, de Graaff et al. 2010, Scheidel, Krausmann 2011, Stoate et al. 2009). The new policy was more concerned with qualitative aspects, such as product quality, food safety and environmental aspects rather than with the quantitative aspects inherent to previous policies (Costantini, Barbetti 2008, Türkekul et al. 2010).

The actual CAP (2014-2020) is raising some concerns due to the downward trend that has been occurring in the allocation of funds to the agricultural sector. In 2007, 50% of the EU budget was allocated to CAP, decreasing to 42% in 2013, and to 35% of the total budget in 2020 (Mylonas 2015, p. 13). Nevertheless, CAP continues to be the largest segment of the EU total budget, allocating 408.31 billion Euros, through two main Pillars (First Pillar 308.73 billion Euros and Second Pillar 99.58 billion Euros in EU funds), during this CAP period. Pillar I provides 'Direct Payments' to farmers guaranteeing farm revenues stabilization and aiming to diminish inequalities in funds attribution among member states. Pillar II supports for long-term 'Rural Development', attempting to modernize the sector, becoming more competitive, maintaining quality and environmental concerns (European Commission 2013, 2016), aiming to more greener and sustainable agriculture, which was not yet achieved (Matthews 2013).

2.3 The Slow Food Movement

In Rome, Italy, in the 1990s, fast food restaurants began to gain a prominent place in the market. In response to the spread of fast food restaurants, a movement arose. The Slow Food Movement started by promoting healthy diets in which olive oil had an important role. This movement soon started to outgrowth convening an international extent and becoming a philosophy of life, encouraging local and sustainable agri-food systems and local food traditions, adjusting food in view of its cultural, social, economic, geographical and environmental contexts through alternative food networks (Ferreira 2009, Goodman, Goodman 2007, Neves et al. 2013). Values that are consistent with the principles of the Mediterranean Diet.

3 The Olive Oil Market

Edaphoclimatic characteristics confine world olive oil production into two zones, between 30 and 45 degrees latitude from both the North and the South hemispheres. Nevertheless, olive oil is produced outside these regions, and production is rising (Pires, Neves 2013).

In the last 25 years under analysis the world production of olive oil has more than doubled (IOC 2015d). The Mediterranean region encompasses the core of the olive oil production (Table 1), which plays an important role in social, economic and environmental terms (Avraamides, Fatta 2008, Muktadirul Bari Chowdhury et al. 2013, Salomone,

Table 1: Olive oil production

| Olive oil | 2015/16 | | 1990/91 | |
Production	Tons	P(%)	Tons	P(%)
Mediterranean countries	2,861,000	95.73	1,400,700	96.40
Europe	2,060,500	68.95	999,200	68.77
European Union	2,049,500	68.58	994,000	68.41
Africa	601,500	20.13	307,500	21.16
Middle East	237,500	7.95	102,500	7.05
South America	42,500	1.42	10,500	0.72
Oceania	18,000	0.60	N/D	N/D
North America	14,000	0.47	1,000	0.07
Other producing countries	14,500	0.49	32,000	2.20
World production	2,988,500	100.00	1,453,000	100.00

Source: IOC (2015b,d)

Ioppolo 2012, Türkekul et al. 2010). This region alone produces 95.7% (2,861,000 of 2,988,500 tons) of the worlds' olive oil, a share that was slightly reduced with the expansion of the production market. In 1990/91, Mediterranean countries were producing 1,400,700 out of 1,453,000 tons, corresponding to 96.4% of total production (IOC 2015d). European Union countries in the North Mediterranean region are the largest producers worldwide with nearly 3/4 of total production (European Commission 2003, Türkekul et al. 2010), a slightly reduced share, given the emergence of other producing countries (Neves, Pires 2013). Currently, European Union is responsible for nearly 69% (2,049,500 tons) of the olive oil production (IOC 2015b).

Spain is the country that produces the most worldwide and since it joined the EU together with Portugal in 1986, olive oil production has experienced a substantial growth. CAP reforms have led to an increase in new plantations and a rise in productivity. This was accomplished by improving growing techniques such as replacing old trees with new ones as well as increasing the number of trees per area (intensive modes of production) and by introducing irrigation to the olive groves production system (Türkekul et al. 2010).

In 1990/91, Spain was the worlds' most productive country with 639,400 tons, 44% of total production (1,453,000 tons). Today, Spain is still the leading producer and has more than doubled its production. With 1,300,000 tons, Spain produces today 43.5% of the worlds' olive oil, a total of 2,988,500 tons (IOC 2015b,d).

Portugal has benefited from the same CAP-EU reforms as Spain, which allowed it to modernize and expand the olive sector, and similarly introducing intensive and irrigated modes of production (INE 2010, Neves et al. 2013, Pires, Neves 2013). Portugal is today the eighth largest producing country of olive oil worldwide and occupies the fourth place within the EU with 82,000 tons. Portugal increased its production more than four times (20,000 tons) since 1990/91 (IOC 2015b,d).

Consumption rose significantly from 1990/91 (1,666,500 tons) until the present time (2,989,000 tons) and, although it mostly occurred in producing countries, it is more widespread than production (Table 2; Figure 1). The Mediterranean region is responsible for about 2/3 of the total consumption of olive oil. In 2015/16, in the Mediterranean region, consumption was expected to represent 65.8% of the world's consumption, which is 1,966,800 of a total of 2,989,000 tons. A much different share compared to 1990/91. At that time 86.7% (1,445,100 tons) were consumed in the region (IOC 2015a,c).

The EU alone was responsible for about 73% of total consumption in 1990/91 (IOC 2015a,c), a share that is becoming lower with the current market's tendency (Figure 1). In 2007/08, slightly more than 2/3 of the total share of olive oil was consumed in the EU (Türkekul et al. 2010). Today it represents just 54% (1,615,000 tons) in relation to total consumption (IOC 2015c). Although the rates are presently lower due to the spreading of markets, consumption is much higher and the general tendency points to a continuous growth in consumption (IOC 2015a,c).

Despite its leading role as world producer, Spain is not the country that consumes the

Table 2: Olive oil consumption

Olive oil Consumption	2015/16		1990/91	
	Tons	P(%)	Tons	P(%)
Mediterranean countries	1,966,800	65.80	1,445,100	86.71
Europe	1,645,500	55.05	1,223,400	73.41
European Union	1,615,000	54.03	1,214,500	72.88
Africa	436,000	14.59	175,500	10.53
Middle East	242,000	8.10	87,000	5.22
North America	346,500	11.59	98,000	5.88
Asia	120,500	4.03	9,000	0.54
South America	94,500	3.16	21,500	1.29
Oceania	37,500	1.25	13,500	0.81
Other prod. countries	11,500	0.38	21,000	1.26
Other non prod. countries	55,000	1.84	21,000	1.26
World consumption	2,989,000	100.00	1,666,500	100.00

Source: (IOC 2015a,c)

most. Italy holds the first place as olive oil consumer for decades. In 1990/91, in Italy, 540,000 tons (32.4%) were being consumed, followed by Spain with 394,100 tons (23.7%). Today, Italy is still the largest consumer worldwide and it is still followed by the world leading producer, Spain, with 580,800 tons (19.4%) and 490,000 tons (16.4%), respectively, of the worlds' consumption. In 1990/91, Portugal was in tenth place consuming 27,000 tons and ranked fifth amongst the EU countries. Today, consumption more than doubled in the country. The 74,000 tons being consumed at present time contributed to the country's rise to the ninth place as world consumer, maintaining the fifth place amongst the EU countries (IOC 2015a,c).

Outside the Mediterranean region, new markets are emerging. The USA is the most prominent while Australia, Brazil, Canada, China, Japan and Russia are also notable markets (European Commission 2012, Salomone, Ioppolo 2012, Türkekul et al. 2010). It is precisely non-producing countries that are consolidating their position in the market as olive oil consumers, explaining the increase in production. Therefore, non-European producing countries in the Mediterranean basin are reinforcing their market share, in some cases, by doubling production in the last 25 years, taking advantage of the stimuli provided by the olive oil sector (IOC 2015d, Mylonas 2015). Despite this, the EU is still responsible for about 2/3 of the world exports and wants to secure that position (Rossi 2017), being the olive oil sector one of the most privileged by CAP, compared to other products such as wine, fruits or vegetables (Mili et al. 2017, Ozden, Dios-Palomares 2016). In 2010/11, exports to third countries reached 447,000 tons, with Spain and Italy contributing the majority share, selling 225,000 and 160,000 tons respectively (European Commission 2012). At the same time, the actual CAP is raising concerns and negative consequences may arise due to expected cuts in subsidies until 2020 (Mylonas 2015, p. 9).

4 Environmental Consequences

While traditional olive groves were once characterized by natural value agricultural systems, recent changes due to the introduction of intensive modes of production have led to negative environmental consequences (De Gennaro et al. 2012, de Graaff et al. 2011, Muktadirul Bari Chowdhury et al. 2013, Ozden, Dios-Palomares 2016).

In Neves, Pires (2013) these consequences are systematized as follows: (i) loss of diversity and landscape modifications; (ii) soil erosion, and; (iii) water consumption and contamination.

Olive trees are highly adaptable to climate in the Mediterranean region (Scheidel, Krausmann 2011) allowing its cultivation in marginal soils, with low fertility (Huang, Sumpio 2008) or in terraces using very low quantities of fertilizers, herbicides and pesticides, characteristic of the traditional olive groves' system (de Graaff et al. 2011,

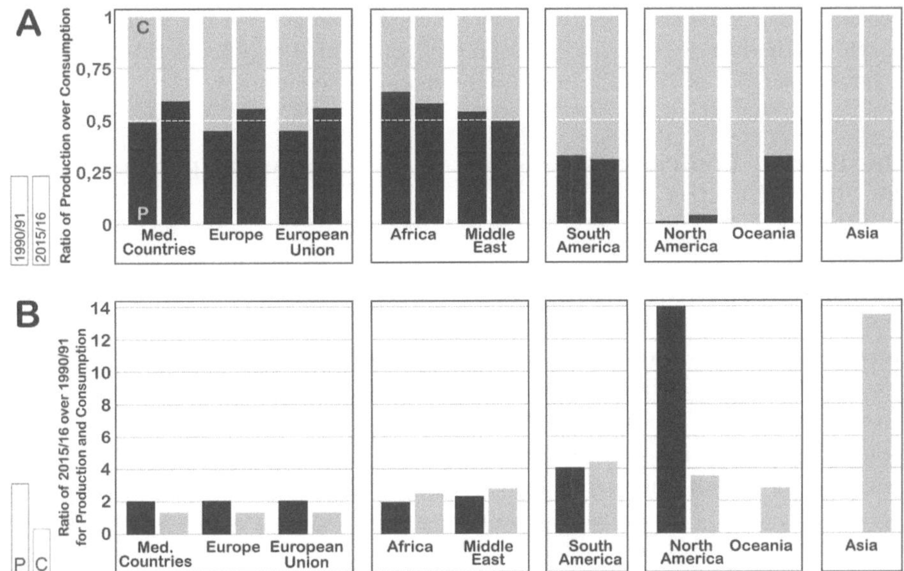

Notes: Notes: P = Production; C = Consumption. Countries in the IOC 2015a,b,c,d were merged by 'region'. Regions were grouped in five blocks according to the following criteria (from left to right): (1) production grew more than consumption; (2) consumption grew more than production; (3) identical production and consumption growth; (4) emerging producing regions that do not yet meet consumers' demand; (5) purely consumer regions.

Figure 1: Dynamics of production and consumption by world regions. (A) Relative weight of production over consumption in 1990/91 and 2015/16 and (B) relative growth in 2015/16 over 1990/91 of production and consumption

Neves, Pires 2013) where spacing between trees (an average of 100 trees per hectare) allows a second crop or pastoralism to be part of a biodiverse landscape (Avraamides, Fatta 2008, European Commission 2012, Ferreira 2010).

Biodiversity loss is highly associated with any crop intensification which adds additional pressures to the environment (Metzidakis et al. 2008). These issues were added to olive groves by shifting farming practices to more intensive modes of production (which can exceed even 2,000 trees per hectare), leading to a transformed landscape with shortened biodiversity (Costantini, Barbetti 2008, Scheidel, Krausmann 2011, Weissteiner et al. 2011).

Intensive monocultures are equally associated with erosion (de Graaff et al. 2011, Salomone, Ioppolo 2012), and according to Beaufoy (2001), the shifting of olive groves to more intensive modes of production not only contributes largely to erosion but it can lead to desertification. Contrary to traditional olive groves that, normally, are not irrigated, intensive and super-intensive olive groves are irrigated. This brought about significant changes in water consumption since these practices are very water-intensive (Avraamides, Fatta 2008, de Graaff et al. 2011).

Environmental problems are not only related to water consumption but also to the high inputs of fertilizers and herbicides used in these intensive modes of production which, in turn, are associated with air, soil and water bodies' contamination (Neves, Pires 2013, Roig et al. 2006, Stroosnijder et al. 2008) and create an encouraging environment to pests and diseases resulting from the excessive use of water (Metzidakis et al. 2008). Rivers in the Mediterranean region have been subject to uncontrolled discharges of olive mill waste (Roig et al. 2006). Dumping olive mill waste was a common practice until the end of the last century, despite its prohibition in the early 1980s. To overcome these issues, new uses have been given to olive mill wastes, such as fertilizer or for the production of bioenergy (Muktadirul Bari Chowdhury et al. 2013, Scheidel, Krausmann 2011). Olive oil extraction systems have also been subject to technological changes. Presently, most olive mills are already equipped with the so-called two-phase olive mill waste. It is more environmentally friendly and needs considerably fewer amounts of water in the olive oil extraction process

(Roig et al. 2006). This technology is now being used in several Mediterranean countries. Spain, which for decades has had serious environmental problems related to olive mill waste, have now 75% of its mills equipped with such technology (IOC 2012).

5 The Iberian Peninsula and reported environmental problems related to the olive oil sector

Olive oil production in its intensive and super-intensive modes of production are related to high rates of erosion in low fertility soils that are now losing biodiversity and introducing great landscape transformations (Vanwalleghem et al. 2010).

Andalusia, Spain, is the most productive region in the world concerning olive groves (Mili et al. 2017). Between 2000 and 2003, the region produced on average 39% of the world's olive oil and 24% of table olives (Gómez et al. 2009).

Today, the Andalusian autonomous community alone, is responsible for 75% of the Spanish olive oil production, which is about 35% of the global production. Despite the region shifting to more sustainable olive oil farming production modes, especially integrated and organic (Mili et al. 2017), it is still facing major problems related to soil loss (Scheidel, Krausmann 2011). In a 2002 study carried out in the Andalusian region, reported topsoil losses in olive groves were on average around 62 tons per hectare/year. Although, in certain areas of the region topsoil losses reached 92 tons per hectare/year. The lowest rate of topsoil losses was estimated at 36 tons per hectare/year. Such rates are considered to be very high compared to soil regeneration rates presented for the region, which vary from one to 12 tons per hectare/year (Scheidel, Krausmann 2011). This issue brought major concerns to the Spanish local government that resulted in the implementation of the National and Andalusian Action Plan against Desertification, meant for the application of good farming practices (Neves, Pires 2013).

In order to better understand the results of the study mentioned above, one must return to the beginning of the 1990s. The region of Andalusia at the beginning of the 1990s was facing periods of droughts and, at the same time, the EU was providing incentives through CAP to increase yields. These constraints and opportunities led to the development of Research and Development programs in a joint initiative from the Andalusian board and private olive producers in 1992. The outcome was the development of a drip irrigation and fertilizer (fertirrigation) system. This system irrigates and fertilizes according to the seasonal needs of the crop. Such technological development is responsible for the increase in productivity and the expansion and intensification (raising the number of trees per hectare) of the olive sector not only in Andalusia but throughout Spain (Scheidel, Krausmann 2011, Vanwalleghem et al. 2010).

Presently, erosion and desertification issues associated to crops' intensification, affect not only the Iberian Peninsula countries but also other Mediterranean countries, namely Greece and Italy (Costantini, Barbetti 2008, DGOTDU 2006, Gómez et al. 2009, Roig et al. 2006). Olive groves' intensive modes of production are being referred to as the most problematic crops concerning these issues (Beaufoy 2001, Neves, Pires 2013, Vanwalleghem et al. 2010).

These environmental problems highlighted an emergent need for solutions. Spain, the world's largest producer, has again and somehow succeeded to properly manage the problems here mentioned. One issue relates to the fact that Spain had exceeded quotas for olive trees and olive oil production, a problem that found an easy and favorable solution among the cross-border regions with the Portuguese territory, namely from the regions of Andalusia and Extremadura. Because Spain had exceeded quotas, the EU was financing the removal of olive trees. At the same time in Portugal, EU was funding the plantation of olive trees. That was done by a considerable number of Spanish olive oil producers. The compensations from removing olive trees from a certain area with exceeded quotas gave them the income necessary to invest in farms in Portugal to plant olive trees and be remunerated for an activity that they are very familiar with. These investors highlight the fact of existing available land and water, particularly in the Alentejo region. A region with high water availability since the construction of the Alqueva dam in 2002, and particularly since it reached its maximum level in 2010. Besides, water, land as well as labor are mentioned to be of lower cost in the Portuguese region comparatively to Spain. These are considered attractive and boosted investment in a time of repealing constraints due to the cross-border situation (Pires, Neves 2013).

By having the biggest artificial lake in Europe, with 250 Sq. km, the Alqueva dam made it possible for the region of Alentejo to expand and transit from traditional to irrigated intensive and super-intensive modes of production. The transition began in the late 1990s, and with the Alqueva irrigation perimeter completely infrastructured and operational today, the olive groves' area is expected to double, and production to significantly increase. Investment is also expected to increase from Andalusia, where water and land resources are pointed as the main reasons (Pires, Neves 2013).

The Alentejo region holds 51% (173,392 hectares in 2011) of the total olive production area, with more than half of the national olive oil being produced here due to the high productivity rates (1,873 kg per hectare), 24% higher than the national average (Neves et al. 2013). Also, note that this region is the second at the EU level with the largest holdings, only surpassed by the Andalusian region, with an average of 7.2 and 8 hectares per holding respectively (European Commission 2012).

6 Discussion and Conclusions

The values associated with the Mediterranean Diet led to its inclusion to the Representative List of the Intangible Cultural Heritage of Humanity. The Mediterranean Diet is, in fact, a way of life with knowledge, traditions, and a remarkable social sense, amongst other values and traditions, visible in many aspects of everyday life of Mediterranean cultures. But this recognition had a "perverse" impact in the sense that the valuation of olive oil, as one of the components of this diet, led to an unprecedented increase in demand in the last decades and, consequently, to its appreciation in the market. This appreciation has stimulated an increased production that was mainly accomplished through agriculture intensification.

The transition from a traditional production mode to intensive and super-intensive modes has altered the landscapes of the Mediterranean olive groves, namely in the Alentejo and Andalusia regions, introducing monotony (large extensions of kilometers only of olive groves) where before existed biodiversity and, above all, having negative environmental impacts in the medium and long terms. Therefore, olive oil should not be reduced to a commodity that is part of a list of consumer products, distinctive of the Mediterranean Diet, which presently is being produced in such a way that few or none meets the values or meaning emphasized by UNESCO.

The same way, the FAO's recognition of the Mediterranean Diet as one of the most sustainable diets can be used to promote olive oil. First of all, it refers to sustainability. As it can be read on their definition, a sustainable diet with low environmental impacts, contributing to a greener economy and respectful of biodiversity. Foremost, olive oil production is not restricted to intensive and super-intensive modes of production, even though, that is the current tendency, which at the same time ends up marginalizing small producers with no ability to compete in the market.

Such tendency benefits from the most recent achievements by FAO and UNESCO based on the Mediterranean Diet, but also from all the previous mentioned campaigns by IOC and EU (namely through the successive CAP) that led to significant changes, reflecting a valorization of olive oil especially in the world market, and raising its demand. A rise that has stimulated production intensification, generally in Northern Mediterranean countries. The intensification in production modes was followed by its mechanization, irrigation and increase of farms' dimensions. Consequently, in the 25 years in analysis, olive oil production has doubled and expanded worldwide and in the Mediterranean region in particular.

Again, one must remind that the current modes of olive oil production are being challenged considering its sustainability. This is particularly accurate in the Iberian Peninsula countries where environmental issues have been here stated and debated. In addition to that, the CAP aims to reduce the direct support to olive oil production, increasing the challenges for the sector.

Acknowledgement

The article was made with the support of CICS.NOVA - Interdisciplinary Centre of Social Sciences of the Universidade Nova de Lisboa, UID/SOC/04647/2 013, with the financial support of FCT/MCTES through National funds.

References

Avraamides M, Fatta D (2008) Resource consumption and emissions from olive oil production: A life cycle inventory case study in Cyprus. *Journal of Cleaner Production* 16[7]: 781–884. CrossRef.

Beaufoy G (2001) EU policies for olive farming, unsustainable on all counts. WWF Europe and BirdLife International

Costantini EAC, Barbetti R (2008) Environmental and visual impact analysis of viticulture and olive tree cultivation in the province of Siena (Italy). *European Journal of Agronomy* 28[3]: 412–426. CrossRef.

De Gennaro B, Notarnicola B, Roselli L, Tassielli G (2012) Innovative olive-growing models: An environmental and economic assessment. Working towards a more sustainable agrifood industry: Main findings from the Food LCA 2010 conference in Bari, Italy, 28

de Graaff J, Duarte F, Fleskens L, de Figueiredo T (2010) The future of olive groves on sloping land and ex-ante assessment of cross compliance for erosion control. *Land Use Policy* 27[1]: 33–41. CrossRef.

de Graaff J, Duran Zuazo VH, Jones N, Fleskens L (2008) Olive production systems on sloping land: Prospects and scenarios. *A Sustainable Future for Olive Production on Sloping Land* 89[2]: 129–139

de Graaff J, Kessler A, Duarte F (2011) Financial consequences of cross-compliance and flat-rate-per-ha subsidies: The case of olive farmers on sloping land. *Land Use Policy* 28[2]: 388–394. CrossRef.

DGOTDU – Direcção-Geral do Ordenamento do Território e Desenvolvimento Urbano (2006) Combate à Desertificação: Orientações para os Planos Regionais de Ordenamento do Território. Direcção-Geral do Ordenamento do Território e Desenvolvimento Urbano, Lisbon, Portugal

European Commission (2003) The olive oil sector in the European Union. European Commission, Agriculture

European Commission (2012) Economic analysis of the olive sector. European Commission, Agriculture and Rural Development

European Commission (2013) Overview of CAP reform 2014-2020 (agricultural policy perspectives brief no. 5). European Commission, Agriculture and Rural Development

European Commission (2016) CAP in your country. European Commission, Agriculture and Rural Development

FAO – Food and Agriculture Organization (2010) Sustainable diets and biodiversity. Directions and solutions for policy, research and action. Food and Agriculture Organization of the United Nations, Rome, Italy. CrossRef.

Ferreira A (2009) The slow food movement. Master Thesis. Faculdade de Ciências da Nutrição e Alimentação, Universidade do Porto, Porto, Portugal

Ferreira D (2010) O olival em modo de produção biológico: Custos e Rentabilidade na região de Moura, Alentejo. Master Thesis. Instituto Superior de Agronomia, Universidade Técnica de Lisboa, Lisbon, Portugal

Gómez JA, Sobrinho T, Giráldez J, E F (2009) Soil management effects on runoff, erosion and soil properties in an olive grove of Southern Spain. *Soil and Tillage Research* 102[1]: 5–13. CrossRef.

Goodman D, Goodman M (2007) Alternative food networks. In: Thrift N, Kitchin R (eds), *International Encyclopedia of Human Geography*, Volume 4. Elsevier, Amsterdam, 208–220

Huang C, Sumpio B (2008) Olive oil, the Mediterranean diet, and cardiovascular health. *Journal of the American College of Surgeons* 207[3]: 407–416. CrossRef.

INE – Instituto Nacional de Estatística (2010) O que mudou na agricultura portuguesa nos últimos dez anos. Recenseamento Agrícola 2009. Dados Preliminares. Instituto Nacional de Estatística, Lisbon, Portugal

IOC – International Olive Council (2012) Policies - Spain. International Olive Council. Retrieved from http://www.internationaloliveoil.org/estaticos/view/136-country-profiles

IOC – International Olive Council (2015a) Olive oils - EU Consumption. International Olive Council. Retrieved from http://www.internationaloliveoil.org/estaticos/view/131-world-olive-oil-figures

IOC – International Olive Council (2015b) Olive oils - EU Production. International Olive Council. Retrieved from http://www.internationaloliveoil.org/estaticos/view/131-world-olive-oil-figures

IOC – International Olive Council (2015c) Olive oils - World Consumption. International Olive Council. Retrieved from http://www.internationaloliveoil.org/estaticos/view/132-world-table-olive-figures

IOC – International Olive Council (2015d) Olive oils - World Production. International Olive Council. Retrieved from http://www.internationaloliveoil.org/estaticos/view/132-world-table-olive-figures

IOC – International Olive Council (n.d.) Mediterranean diet pyramid. International Olive Council. Retrieved from http://www.internationaloliveoil.org/estaticos/view/87-mediterranean-diet-pyramid

Matthews A (2013) Greening agricultural payments in the EU's common agricultural policy. *Bio-Based and Applied Economics Journal* 2[1]: 27

Metzidakis I, Martinez-Vilela A, Castro Nieto G, Basso B (2008) Intensive olive orchards on sloping land: Good water and pest management are essential. *A Sustainable Future for Olive Production on Sloping Land* 89[2]: 120–128

Mili S, Judez L, De Andres R (2017) Investigating the impacts of EU CAP reform 2014-20 and developments in sustainable olive farming systems. *New Medit* 16[3]: 2–10

Moro E (2016) The Mediterranean diet from Ancel Keys to the UNESCO cultural heritage. A pattern of sustainable development between myth and reality. 2nd international symposium 'New Metropolitan Perspectives' - strategic planning, spatial planning, economic programs and decision support tools, through the implementation of Horizon/Europe2020. ISTH2020, Reggio Calabria (Italy), 18-20 May 2016, 223, 655-661

Muktadirul Bari Chowdhury AKM, Akratos CS, Vayenas DV, Pavlou S (2013) Olive mill waste composting: A review. *International Biodeterioration & Biodegradation* 85: 108–119

Mylonas P (2015) Olive oil: Establishing the Greek brand (sectoral report). National Bank of Greece, economic analysis department

Neves B, Pires IM (2013) The impact of agricultural policies and growing investment in olive sector in the Alentejo region. Políticas de Base e Recuperação Económica. Universidade do Minho, Braga, Portugal

Neves B, Pires IM, Roxo MJ (2013) Culturas intensivas e superintensivas e a susceptibilidade à Desertificação: o caso do olival no Alentejo. In: Correia T, Henriques V, Julião R (eds), *Geografia: Espaço, Natureza, Sociedade e Ciência*. Associação Portuguesa de Geógrafos, Évora, Portugal, 44–51

Ozden A, Dios-Palomares R (2016) Is the olive oil an efficient sector? A meta frontier analysis considering the ownership structure. *New Medit* 15[3]: 2–9

Pires IM, Neves B (2013) From periphery to Euroregion: Foreign investment in olive groves in an Alentejo in times of change. Place-based policies and economic recovery. Universidade do Minho, Braga, Portugal

Roig A, Cayuela ML, Sánchez-Monedero MA (2006) An overview on olive mill wastes and their valorisation methods. *Waste Management* 26[9]: 960–969. CrossRef.

Rossi R (2017) The EU olive and olive oil sector. Main features, challenges and prospects. Members' research service no. PE 608.690, p. 12. European Parliamentary Research Service, European Parliament

Salomone R, Ioppolo G (2012) Environmental impacts of olive oil production: A life cycle assessment case study in the province of Messina (Sicily). Working towards a more sustainable agri-food industry: Main findings from the Food LCA 2010 conference in Bari, Italy, 28, 88-100

Scheidel A, Krausmann F (2011) Diet, trade and land use: A socio-ecological analysis of the transformation of the olive oil system. *Land Use Policy* 28: 47–56. CrossRef.

Stoate C, Báldi A, Beja P, Boatman ND, Herzon I, van Doorn A, de Snoo GR, Rakosy L, Ramwell C (2009) Ecological impacts of early 21st century agricultural change in Europe – A review. *Journal of Environmental Management* 91[1]: 22–46. CrossRef.

Stroosnijder L, Mansinho MI, Palese AM (2008) OLIVERO: The project analysing the future of olive production systems on sloping land in the Mediterranean basin. *A Sustainable Future for Olive Production on Sloping Land* 89[2]: 75–85

Türkekul B, Günden C, Abay C, Miran B (2010) Competitiveness of Mediterranean countries in the olive oil market. *New Medit* 9[1]: 41–46

UNESCO – United Nations Educational, Scientific and Cultural Organization (2013a) Decisions. UNESCO, Baku, Azerbaijan

UNESCO – United Nations Educational, Scientific and Cultural Organization (2013b) Nomination file no. 00884 for inscription in 2013 on the Representative List of the Intangible Cultural Heritage of Humanity. UNESCO, Baku, Azerbaijan

Vanwalleghem T, Laguna A, Giráldez JV, Jiménez-Hornero FJ (2010) Applying a simple methodology to assess historical soil erosion in olive orchards. *Geomorphology* 114[3]: 294–302. CrossRef.

Weissteiner C, Strobl P, Sommer S (2011) Assessment of status and trends of olive farming intensity in U-Mediterranean countries using remote sensing time series and land cover data. *Ecological Indicators* 11[2]: 601–610. CrossRef.